X

MAKING THE CASE FOR YOUR LIBRA

A How-To-Do-It Manual

Sally Gardner Reed

HOW-TO-DO-IT MANUALS
FOR LIBRARIANS

NUMBER 104

NEAL-SCHUMAN PUBLISHERS, INC.
New York, London

Published by Neal-Schuman Publishers, Inc.
100 Varick Street
New York, NY 10013

The paper used in this publication meets the minimum requirements of American National Standard for Information Sciences—Permanence of Paper for Printed Library Materials, ANSI Z39.48–1992.

Printed and bound in the United States of America.

ISBN 1–55570–399–2

Library of Congress Cataloging-in-Publication Data

Reed, Sally Gardner, 1953–
 Making the case for your library : a how-to-do-it manual / Sally Gardner Reed.
  p. cm. — (How-to-do-it manuals for librarians ; no. 104)
 ISBN 1–55570–399–2 (alk. paper)
 1. Libraries—Public relations—United States—Handbooks manuals, etc. 2. Library fund raising—United States—Handbooks, manuals, etc. 3. Library finance—United States—Handbooks, manuals, etc. I. Title. II. How-to-do-it manuals for libraries ; no. 104.

Z716.3 .R43 2000
025.1'1—dc21   00-061297

For Hal

CONTENTS

    Measuring Success   137
    Keep Your Eyes on the Prize   139

    Index   141

    About the Author   143

LIST OF FIGURES
AND CREDITS

PREFACE

Political power—today it's a necessary ingredient for library survival. In our rapidly changing environment we must position libraries so they are seen as the central entity for providing access to the full spectrum of information, knowledge, ideas, programs, and services that support individual learning and intellectual growth. We librarians may take this view as a given but those who fund us often do not. While this is an age-old problem, we are facing increasing questions about the relevance of libraries in the new digital age. We must be able to anticipate and address these questions in a compelling and powerful way.

We can no longer feel confident that political authorities will automatically view libraries as important and, therefore, provide them with full financial support. Some say the library is an endangered species. If we librarians cannot show community and campus leaders how libraries are relevant now and for the future, we will continue to be marginalized, outsourced, privatized, and eventually closed altogether. If we fail to make the case that libraries are central to a democracy, to individual learning, and ultimately to our future well-being as a nation, then access to knowledge may well become not an entitlement, but a privilege for those who can afford it.

I believe that most librarians now realize that advocacy is an important component of their jobs, but I'm not convinced that we have begun to communicate in a politically powerful way with our patrons, our supporters, and those who hold our purse strings. We can't do our jobs without the political and financial support of our administration and governors. Many librarians have developed excellent marketing materials and campaigns, but too often these tools describe library services while they fail to convey the *importance* of libraries.

Making the Case for Your Library demonstrates how librarians across the country can help their libraries not just survive, but thrive, by developing pervasive public relations materials. I wrote this book to show how librarians can communicate not just *what* their library is doing, but *why* it matters. This is a crucial distinction. When you develop marketing materials focused on the "what," you are typically looking for more users as an outcome. When you focus on "why it matters," you expand your public relations reach beyond potential users to potential supporters—and there is a difference.

Think of all the times and all the ways you promote your library and its services. In doing so, do you focus on quality services, access to a wide variety of resources, and a skilled, caring staff? Do you work hard to let your audience know when important events or programs are happening and what new materials are available? If you answered "yes" to these questions, you are typical. But how often do you use all the opportunities for promotion to make a *politically powerful* case for your library? Do you ensure that every time you inform your public about library services you also let them know *why* it matters? And not just why it matters in general (i.e., libraries are good), but why libraries matter to everyone in the community, even those who don't use the library.

The value of making the case for your library's services even if you do not recruit new users was made quite clear to me several years ago. I was attending a Rotary Club meeting and the day's speaker was the director of the public bus service in our town. All of us in the audience were convinced we were in for a fairly boring presentation since not one of us rode public buses and did not imagine we would any time in the near future. This man, however, knew his audience, and because he knew he was not talking to customers or potential customers he did not discuss timely schedules, clean buses, low-cost rides, or friendly service—even though I'm sure he could have bragged about all of that. No, this man painted a picture of what life would be like for us, his audience, without good effective bus service in our town. He talked about how many more cars there would be on the road if bus service disappeared. He talked about additional parking lots and their costs, and about the increase in traffic cops if more drivers hit the roads. He talked about emissions and our environment. He talked about how public bus service mattered to *us*!

To show how librarians are using their promotional efforts to focus on the "why" as well as the "what," I began collecting materials at the American Library Association's "Swap 'N' Shop." This is a wonderful event, held at each annual ALA conference, allowing librarians of all types to share their best promotional materials while discovering new ways to get their message and information across to their respective communities. What I found, by and large, was an assortment of creative materials designed to promote (primarily) public library use. Precious few of these brochures, bookmarks, newsletters, calendars, flyers, and reports, however, included statements, essays, or articles on why the services they were promoting make a difference to both the people who use them and the people who don't.

It occurred to me then that librarians who are already very savvy at marketing their services were just one short step away from using these same vehicles to promote the importance of libraries in a powerful, ongoing way. We are already designing, developing, and publishing materials for our public. Why not use these same materials to be more politically effective? Instead of just focusing on increasing use, why not focus on increasing support as well?

Making the Case for Your Library features samples of marketing and promotional materials from libraries that have taken that last step—telling their communities what they have and why it matters. Most of the samples come from public libraries, because they are leading the way for the political marketing of their systems but their work is easily transferable to academic and school library promotions. In looking at the samples, it will be clear that the size of the library doesn't matter. You will see politically savvy samples from such small libraries as the Ela Area Public Library in Lake Zurich, Illinois, and the Bedford County Public Library in Virginia to such large library systems as the Kings County (Wash.) Library System and the Queens Borough (N.Y.) Public Library.

This book will show you how to use traditional promotional materials and techniques to make your library and its services matter to everyone in your community, public or academic, whether they use your library or not. If you garner more users in the process, you will have expanded your support base and will have made your library more directly meaningful to more people. In the end, providing all those excellent services that you wish to promote will depend on your ability to garner support and financial resources from the powers that be, and many of these folks, all too often, will never set foot inside your library's doors.

And you must know how to use the support you've generated on a continuing basis to win support in a campaign that is targeted toward achieving a specific goal.

If ever libraries existed happily apart from the political world in which they exist, they do not now. Libraries must compete effectively for resources that are in increasing demand, and we must constantly combat the mistaken common belief that the new information technology makes libraries *less* important (when, in fact, it makes libraries *more* important than ever before). It is no longer possible to get adequate funding simply by pointing out the inherent good of libraries. A passive approach just won't work.

In our rapidly changing and highly competitive environment, every library director needs to make a good, strong case for the library. If we are successful in developing and selling our message at the local level, we can ensure that we get both the funding we need to deliver services and a political power base to ensure library-friendly public policy. It's not just about the money anymore, it's also about developing support that can influence information policy and legislation at the state and national level. This is a job that must enlist the help of trustees, patrons, students, faculty, supporters, alumni, and Friends of the Library. It's a job that must be ongoing and aggressive.

Technological advances, demographic shifts, and economic changes all impact libraries and challenge our relevance as well as threaten our ability to deliver viable services. We need to develop a strong commitment to library funding and a seminal role in setting information policy. It is ironic that libraries today seem to have no more political clout than they did decades ago, despite the critical role we play today on campuses and in communities. More than ever, we need to develop power and influence within our larger organizations (be that the campus, the corporation, or the community) and we need to become key and respected players in the larger national legislative arena as well.

Ask any librarian why he or she entered the profession and you are not likely to hear that the opportunity to become involved in politics and power struggles were key attractions. Yet, political advocacy is critical to us now and it is a role that we are, in fact, well equipped to assume. We have the political tools at hand, what we need to do is learn how to use them effectively.

You *can* make the case for your library—in fact, you can do it in a way that will generate enthusiasm and active support from library users and community leaders. This book will show you how to be successful within any kind of library community—public, school, corporate, or academic. Librarians are not newcomers to promoting their services; what we've been less successful doing is ensuring that our promotions and communications are politically powerful as well.

Making an effective case for your library requires you to develop a strong message that conveys what your library's mission is and why that mission is important to the larger organization. After developing that message, you need to share it—you need to work to ensure that your entire community has heard the message and supports it. *Making the Case for Your Library* is divided into three parts. Part I discusses ways to develop and share a politically powerful message. Parts II and III show how to put your message into action. Specifically, Part II focuses on the ongoing campaign for support—how to keep your library's profile high and viewed as important by the decision makers in your community or on your campus. Part III discusses how to develop an effect campaign for a specific purpose, such as passing a bond referendum or getting a significant increase in your operating budget. In these two parts, you will find samples of library promotional materials that send a powerful message for support. You will find instructions for speaking with the media and speaking to groups that can help the library. You will learn how to handle tough questions and concerns that could potentially damage support for your library.

Being an effective advocate for libraries may be one of the most important roles for today's librarian. It is no longer a role that can be successfully played once a year at budget time; it must become a part of everything we do, every message we send. These are exciting and perhaps even scary times, but if you became a librarian to make a difference, the opportunity to do so has never been greater.

ACKNOWLEDGMENTS

I would like to thank the Norfolk Public Library Board of Trustees and the Friends of the Norfolk Public Library for their commitment and dedication in running an excellent "1 % for Libraries" campaign and for never giving up. I would also like to thank Beth Nawalinski, Public Information Specialist at the Norfolk Public Library, for her invaluable advice and assistance in putting this book together. Finally, I would like to thank Michael Kelley of Neal-Schuman Publishers for his good humor and tenacity!

PART I

DEVELOPING AND SHARING
THE MESSAGE

1 DEVELOPING YOUR LIBRARY'S MESSAGE

To be effective, your message must be:

- Politically powerful
- Focused on desired outcome
- Simple and repeatable
- Flexible and adaptable to different audiences

To be effective at delivering a good, strong message to decision makers, you must have—you've got it!—a good strong message. "The message" is really a tool. If you're really clever you might develop it into a motto, but the real value of the message is to keep all of your public relations, professional interactions, and negotiations focused on achieving your goal. Whatever you develop as your message, it should be politically powerful and focused on desired outcome. It should also be simple enough that it becomes "repeatable" by staff, by supporters, and eventually, by others within the organization; and it should be flexible enough to be adapted to all audiences and their concerns.

THE POLITICALLY POWERFUL MESSAGE

The most important question to keep in mind as you are crafting a politically powerful message is, "Why does it matter?" The answer to that question should be embedded in the message. "Libraries are good." "Libraries are important." "Libraries serve everyone." "Libraries provide access to information." "Libraries support lifelong learning." These are all true statements, but they don't answer the most important question. "Why it matters" is not obvious to everyone.

The only way to develop a message that resonates with the powers that be in your community (be it academic, school, or public) is to make it clear that the service the library provides is important to them and their mission. It's about relevance. How would the absence of the library affect the community? What do you contribute that is indispensable? Why are libraries good? Why are libraries important? How does serving everyone make a difference? How are libraries unique in providing access to information and why is that important? Why does lifelong learning matter?

In addition to answering such questions, the message should be responsive to the priorities of those who control our current and future viability. A college or university wants to be seen as a leader in its field, in order to attract the best students, teachers, researchers, and funding. Most communities want to be economically healthy and perceived to offer the highest possible quality of life for their citizens. In both of these cases, the politically effective message must show how the library is a critical component of the success of these quests.

Answering the question of why libraries matter becomes easier when viewed through the lens of a broader set of priorities. For example, in the academic environment the library often uses cutting-edge technology to provide students and faculty with the resources they need to excel. The campus library can be the most public (and promotable) symbol of the quality of education, research, and commitment to learning that the school offers—attracting not only future students and faculty but funding as well. Academic scholarship depends on the traditional notion that our knowledge base is evolutionary and built on centuries of thought, research, and the written record. Nowhere does this traditional foundation meet with technologically avant-garde methods of accessing information more than in the library. Without the library, the critical nexus between the records and knowledge of the past and the information technology of the future would be lost. It is a nexus that practically defines 21st century education, and it is embodied by the library.

For many cities and towns across the country, the ultimate goal is to achieve the economic health necessary to provide excellent quality of life. Usually, high quality of life is defined by good jobs, excellent educational opportunities, enjoyable and accessible recreation, clean environment, low poverty, and access to good health care. It is tempting for libraries to show how they represent several of the outcomes, such as good education and recreation, and how good libraries contribute to quality of life. What is politically more powerful, however, is to show how a library supports the achievement of the desired outcomes altogether. That is, how do libraries contribute to the economic vitality of the city; an economic vitality that makes all other outcomes affordable and, therefore, possible. If you can show this in the message, you are showing that libraries are part of the big picture solution and not just one of the consequences of a good economy or just one component of good quality of life.

FOCUS ON DESIRED OUTCOME

As you contemplate "the message" you should be sure that you are focused on outcome. What are you trying to achieve? If you are seeking a more active and respected role in setting information policy, then your message should focus on librarians as the information experts in a rapidly changing electronic environment. If you are seeking better funding to keep up with this changing environment, then your message should convey the increasingly indispensable role that the library plays in the institution's or the community's competitiveness and strength. A generic message will, at best, get you generic results. Messages that generally reiterate the intrinsic value of libraries end up being the kind of "mom and apple pie" messages that libraries have relied on in the past. Not very political—not very powerful.

The clearer you are in your own mind about what you are trying to achieve, the more likely you are to develop a message powerful enough to help you achieve it. Again, it is not enough to simply deliver a "feel good" message about the library. The message must say what the library needs to succeed in its critical role in the community or organization.

BE SIMPLE AND REPEATABLE

The message should be simple. You'll know you've succeeded in developing a simple but strong message when you hear someone generally believed to be outside the library circles repeating it—and if you have a clear message and promote it well (more on that subject in Part II) this will happen. Remember "It's the economy, stupid"? That message was originally developed as a reminder by former President Bill Clinton's campaign staff to stay focused in developing his message, but it was so simple and so strong that it became universally known and used. If your message is designed, for example, to ensure that you play a lead role as information policy is being developed in your organization, then your message may be as simple as, "Today's librarians are *the* experts in the information revolution." Okay, maybe not as catchy as Clinton's, but your message is not (probably) something you put on your stationery—it's what keeps you focused as you work to influence others.

Simplicity of message also helps to ensure that your staff and library supporters all stay on the same page when interacting with those who influence the direction the library and its services take. Speaking with one voice is powerful in itself. If your message is not clear and strong, developed and supported by staff, it is likely to be rendered ineffective as it becomes misinterpreted or even reinvented by some of your (potentially at least) best allies.

FLEXIBILITY AND ADAPTABILITY

Finally, you should be able to adapt your message to whatever audience you're engaging. This is important. If I were to single out the one major mistake librarians make in trying to persuade others to support libraries it is that we forget that other people have other agendas. Sadly and too often, the people who have the most influence over our future are really not all that interested in libraries. This divergence can be changed—it's what power and influence are all about. The trick is to link what's important to your library (the message) with what's important to them. If your dean, for example, has the most influence over your library's budget and money is your message, then you must learn what is important to your dean. If it's increased enrollment, then make the case that high-tech, state-of-the-art information services are critical to attracting today's students. If your dean is interested in "bragging rights," be sure you let him or her know that cutting-edge libraries are drawing national attention.

The same concept is true for public libraries. What is your city or town manager most interested in? Education? Tourism? Economic development? If you give it some thought, you will find a way to show how libraries support the city's agenda. In delivering the message, it's not about what you want, it's about what others want—*know your audience*.

In addition, your message must resonate with those people who can influence the decision makers in your community. It is important that you, as the expert on library and information matters, are able to connect directly with decision makers, but it is equally and maybe even more important that you connect well with those who have influence over those who ultimately determine the library's fate. These may be people who have influence by sheer numbers (alumni, parents, citizens, Friends), or they may be a small cadre of individuals who wield influence one-on-one with those who make decisions, such as faculty leaders, others in the administration, community leaders, and/or business leaders. The message must be compelling to them as well and powerful enough to move them to action on the library's behalf. Ultimately, it won't be the message itself that makes the case for your library but how it is employed.

PUTTING IT ALL TOGETHER

It may seem impossible: develop a message that is politically powerful, that conveys why the library matters, that is focused on achieving a specific goal, that is simple and repeatable, and that can be adapted to a wide variety of audiences. The good news is that libraries *do* matter, they *are* important, and they *are* indispensable, so developing a good strong message will be easier than you think.

What do you want? If it is funding then think about your environment, what is important to the leadership, and how the library will help achieve it. Let's look again at competitiveness for an academic environment. How about a message that says "The John Smith Library is both the symbol and the center for 21st century education on our campus—bringing the knowledge of the past together with the information technology of the future, keeping our college competitive. 21st century libraries require 21st century funding." This message is specific about this campus's library. It says that the library symbolizes the college's commitment to knowledge past and future. It says that the library is central to the academic mission. And finally, it says the funding is necessary to achieve and maintain the library's ability to meet that mission.

What is important about this particular message is that the last sentence can be omitted; library staff can use the first sentence alone to promote just "the importance of the library." The Friends and supporters of the library, however, can add the last sentence to their advocacy efforts to bring the final important concept home to those who ultimately fund the library. The tag line "21st century libraries require 21st century funding" is simple and repeatable. It's an easy message for advocates to send in a consistent manner and, together with the message of why it matters, it can be a tool for a powerful campaign.

The same concept can work for public libraries as well. What matters most to your community? Perhaps your city or town is focusing on literacy. This is a critical area for job growth, diminishment of welfare roles, economic development, and overall quality of life. The public library can and does play a central role in supporting literacy at all stages of life—from cradle to grave. The message the public library sends should convey the importance and effectiveness of its services in providing support for literacy—all types of services and for all people.

A simple message such as "Libraries = Literacy, It's Time to Thrive" is strong and repeatable and can give you a launch point to "sell" the unique and indispensable services that are critical to a well-informed, well-educated community. The theme of "literacy" in its broadest form can be used to incorporate the importance of all library services and show how they support the greater good of the community and, ultimately, of the nation.

2 SHARING THE MESSAGE

The case for the library gains strength when you get others, including:

- Staff
- Trustees
- Friends
- Patrons
- Community at large
- Community and campus leaders

on board to share the message. If anyone running for office anywhere in America had the loyal following that libraries do, that candidate would rejoice—and win! The potential we have in the "passive" advocates in the library and throughout the organization is staggering. Our job is to turn passive support into active support. You are not, in all probability, going to increase the power and influence you and your library have single-handedly. It's important that you present your message as often and compellingly as possible, and in as many venues as possible, with the goal of bringing others on board to speak out for your library.

Once you have developed the message, it will be very easy to weave it into every public relations opportunity—opportunities that you may need to create (more on that in Part II). For example, if your library has a newsletter you have the power of the press at your disposal. Typically, newsletters are used to communicate upcoming events, new acquisitions, and items of interest to library users—the standard approach is to inform, not to influence. Time to change the approach. You don't need to change what you include, but to be more powerful, you should include why everything you do *matters*. If you are touting a new program, explain in terms of your message why it matters—show what difference it makes to your institution or your community and its goals. Show how the library is a key player in the achievement of those goals.

Creating a strong base of support requires that all constituents be well informed about your goals and what it will take to achieve them. Further, they have to know how they can help. Depending on your own political environment, you (or a Friends group or a Board of Trustees) should stay in constant touch with the constituents and, when necessary, be very clear and blunt about how they can help. Look around and decide who holds the most sway over decision makers and target that influential group. If it is alumni, send out a special newsletter using your message to encourage them to influence the administration. Similarly, an annual newsletter to parents could be an extremely powerful instrument to influence those who have power over the library. In the public library, trustees and Friends can develop postcard campaigns to the general public and circulate petitions showing grassroots support for the library and its needs. Be clear about your message, be clear about what library supporters can do to help, and be clear about why the library matters to them.

Studies have shown that as a group librarians typically aren't extroverts, but assertiveness is critical to the establishment of power within the organization. Assertiveness can be difficult for shy people, but it does get easier with practice, and nothing will sell like our own passion and belief in why we're important. Though a powerful campaign to make the case for your library must include active support from constituents and influential leaders, it begins with you. You will have to motivate your trustees and Friends to wage the campaign on behalf of the library. You will have to network with those who have power and influence in your community to bring them on board.

Luckily, most libraries are not new to the world of promotion. Libraries typically publish newsletters and program flyers, send out press releases, and present programs to civic and campus organizations. It is likely that these methods of promotion are designed to *inform* patrons and potential patrons of library offerings, but they can easily be transformed into vehicles for letting those who need and use libraries understand why library services matter and what they can do to help support this valuable institution.

GET "OUTSIDERS" ON BOARD

The best library advocates are those with no obvious self-interest. I say "obvious" because I believe that everyone has an interest in keeping libraries of all types well supported. Clearly, if we are to be a self-governing nation, individuals must have access to information and learning throughout a lifetime. Libraries are unique in offering individual access to information, ideas, and learning opportunities on their own terms and in their own time. Even people who do not use libraries benefit by their very presence. Archibald MacLeish said, "What is more important in a library than anything else—than everything else—is the fact that it exists." Imagine what our country, or any democracy, might be like without libraries.

The message about the importance of libraries is ultimately the one we want to share with everyone. It'll be a great day when libraries are seen as critical to our democracy and quality of life as those institutions that support public safety, economic development, formal education, health care, and our justice system, because, of course, libraries are important contributors to all these areas. When the importance of libraries (your library!) is fully understood by those who fund us and those who set policies that affect our ability to provide service, our battles will be fewer and smaller.

In the meantime, those who are not directly associated with libraries or with your library are often the ones with the most credibility in getting the message across. Your job, then, is to develop, nurture, and educate a cadre of library supporters who can be articulate spokespeople for the cause. Doing this takes time and energy (and it's an ongoing endeavor), but the dividends can be tremendous when the time comes for you to deploy them on the library's behalf.

USE YOUR FIRST, BEST TOOL—YOU!

Networking should be on the list of job qualifications for any library administrator. If you are reading this book, you care about making the case for your library. Nothing can replace you as your library's number one spokesperson. You know how important your library is to your community or campus. You know what is needed to provide services, both in terms of funding and policy. You are the best person to begin the work of building external library support. Be a leader!

There are probably many opportunities to network with people who have influence in your community or on campus. You may well have to identify those opportunities and insinuate yourself into them—especially if you have been spending most of your time working only within the walls of your library. Get out! Now! Join a civic organization that has influential members. Get involved in high-profile projects in your community or on campus, especially those that have no obvious link to libraries.

A highly effective way to become regarded as a "leader" in your larger organization is to become *actively* involved in committees or task forces. Ask for an assignment within your local government or on campus with a committee that is doing important work. It is especially effective to work on a committee that has no direct relationship to libraries. This is a long-term effort to increase your credibility and profile. It is important to be productive in whatever assignment you get and to be seen by those working with you as someone who is knowledgeable, dependable, and clearly an achiever. The more you are seen as a leader within your organization and a team player, the more your voice will be respected when you return to your role as a library advocate. Too often, we make the mistake of only being seen or heard when the library needs something. This strategy not only lacks power, it can even be counterproductive. By speaking out only at budget time, you may be seen as a whiner or beggar and not as someone who has the overall interests of the larger organization at heart and who sees excellent library services as an important way for the organization to achieve its goals.

In addition to committee work, ask for opportunities to speak about the library and library services at venues where there will be influential people. Be assertive. There are *always* opportunities to speak out if you look for them. Consider how what the library is doing meshes with the issues of other campus or community organizations, and ask to share your perspectives with those groups. Civic organizations are always looking for speakers and they would certainly welcome a call from you offering to present library issues to them. Once you get any speaking engagement, however, it is critical that you make a powerful presentation that will continue to enhance your reputation as a leader and that will ensure your audience leaves with your message in mind. In the end, making a powerful presentation is a lot easier than most people think (see Chapter 4).

Even if you'd rather not, respond to those pro forma invitations you receive by virtue of your position. Once you get the opportunity to meet and greet or the opportunity to speak about libraries, be sure you have your message in mind and don't lose the opportunity to make whatever you say about your library politically powerful. Networking is a critical component to your ability to be a library leader. Clearly, people listen and respond more to those with whom they've established a relationship—be that business or social. Don't miss opportunities to get to know on a personal basis those people on campus or in your community who are the "movers and shakers." You will need them on board to wage an effective campaign on behalf of your library and you will be able to bring them on board if you know them personally.

For those one-on-one networking opportunities, the best advice is to know your message and don't be shy. When people ask about your library and its services, let them know how proud you are to be a librarian, why what your library does matters, and, if the conversation heads that way, how they can help. Don't whine about a lack of funding, support, or respect (it's tempting, I know). Instead, be positive about the library and when people show some real interest, let them know you'd enjoy sounding them out about their views on library services and how they think you might better promote the library. At the very least, remember names of those who may be inclined to help you in the future.

DOES IMAGE MATTER?

With all my heart, I wish I could say that image does not matter. The fact is, image matters very much—especially initially. It would be wonderful if we lived in a world where all people were judged solely by the "content of their character." Unless we project a professional, confident, and accessible image, however, the people that matter most to the library may never take the time to get to know us. We may lose the opportunity to make an important connection if we come across as frumpy, staid, stodgy, or unsophisticated (pick the traditional, librarian-describing adjective of your choice).

One cliché that sticks with me in all my advocacy efforts is that "a bank won't lend you money until you can prove that you don't need it." It's an amazingly paradoxical concept, but so often it's true. I have found that "need" alone is a very difficult sell in getting support. Another cliché that is equally true and the other side of this same coin is that "success breeds success." People often don't *support* as much as they *invest* in you and your cause (the library). This tendency is as true in garnering political support as it is in fund raising. After all, what you are really asking is for people to spend political capital in supporting the library and its agenda.

For this reason it is important for you and your library's services to look as polished and sophisticated as possible. Just as you personally want to portray a highly professional image, the library's image should be professional, too. Be sure that your materials are attractive and professional—work hard to create an image that attracts the powerful support that you need. You want to position your library as an important cause, not as a favored charity. Image does matter.

WORK WITH YOUR STAFF

The best laid advocacy plans cannot succeed without the buy-in and support of the library staff. First of all, excellent public service is one of the best tools you have to generate support. Second, the staff should share your goals for advocacy so they can help you send the message. With the staff on board, you have your first coalition for support. They are the front line in the campaign and can be an excellent source of both moral support and actual political support.

The best way to bring your staff in is to include them in the planning. They are the ones interacting on a daily basis with your patrons. They are likely to know best what will "sell" with the patrons and what will motivate their support. If, for example, you design a building campaign around the concept of enhanced access to computer technology when the patrons have been complaining about the lack of books and audiovisual materials, you are likely to miss these patrons as a target for support altogether. Even though building facilities that can accommodate computer technology is a must, you would be more successful in this case to pitch the need to these patrons based on more space for shelving to enlarge the book and audiovisual collections. As discussed earlier, you need to know your audience—and when your audience is your patronage, your staff will be your best resource to finding out what matters to them.

In addition to being able to offer valuable insight for planning the campaign message, the staff will be highly effective in delivering that message if they understand it, have helped create it, and agree with it. Without including your staff in your advocacy efforts, you can't be sure that you are all speaking with one voice and that you are all working toward the same goal. Never underestimate the power of your staff as political allies—they can help . . . or hurt.

Finally, as simple as it sounds, the quality of public service is an absolutely critical component for generating grassroots support. No matter how legitimate your case or how effective you are in making the case, the grassroots will not support any agency that fails to deliver good public service. Similarly, it is much easier to convince people to support the library and take action on behalf of the library if they feel kinship and loyalty to you. This kind of association is almost always the by-product of good service. Be sure that when you work with staff to generate and then implement an advocacy campaign, they understand how important the quality of their service is to the success of that campaign. Customer service training should always be a high, ongoing priority for you and your staff, but never more so than when you are trying to make the case for your library.

WORK WITH YOUR BOARD

If you have a Board of Trustees, whether governing or advisory, you have a group tailor-made to become the library's most vocal and visible advocates. Be sure that you work with your board to let them know that this is an important role for them. If in the past they have been of the quiet, rubber-stamp variety, it's important to convince them that this new role is critical and definitely more important than anything else they can do to support the library.

In the best of cases, the board is already comprised of influential people. If not, it may be difficult and awkward for you to work toward changing that. However, if even one member is politically connected as well as politically savvy, it may be time for you to take that member out to lunch to talk about ways in which you can create a more actively political board. Perhaps attrition will allow you the opportunity to suggest someone with good political connections (and if you've been doing a good job at networking, you have a name ready of someone interested and able).

Even a board comprised of "regular" folks will be able to help you get the word out, either through an ongoing communications plan or through a targeted campaign to gain support for the library. The first step is for the board to understand this as its role. You can and should guide them in the development of a campaign strategy or a communication plan, but it is very important that you get them to agree to act.

Any board will be more willing to become active and be better at doing so if they, too, know the message, or, better yet, if they've had a hand in developing it. Inviting participation and brainstorming in developing the library's message will certainly engage even the most passive boards. Having "lay" people help develop your message will not only bring them along to a more active role, but it will also make the message meaningful to people who are not already intimately involved in the library.

In addition to helping to develop the message, the board should be actively involved in helping to send it. Whether your message is part of an ongoing communications plan or part of a campaign designed to target a specific outcome, it is likely that your board will have more authority and more credibility in delivering the message than staff because they are less likely to be perceived as acting out of self-interest. Just as it's important for librarians to network on behalf of the library, the trustees should be encouraged to do so as well. Your board is obviously made up of individuals who have a sense of responsibility for being involved in some kind of community service. It is highly likely that these people also are involved in other community, civic, or campus organizations as well and they could easily carry the message with them into other venues.

In a more targeted campaign, the trustees should be encouraged to create opportunities to speak out on behalf of the library. Knowing the message will make it easier for them, and promotional materials to support the campaign will also be a tremendous help, especially for those trustees unaccustomed to public speaking or to aggressive promotion of a cause (see Parts II and III).

Another important role for the trustees is to identify those special people on campus or in the community who have significant authority over library funding or policy. Sometimes the most effective political work is one-on-one. The right library advocate speaking with the right VIP. If no one on your board is close to or has influence with those who make important decisions affecting your library, board members should think about who *does* have that kind of influence and work to make a connection that way.

Even if, in the end, the trustees just do not have connections with the powers that be—either directly or indirectly—they still should be encouraged to phone or visit key leaders and let them know how important library services are and what kind of support is needed to ensure that quality services continue. The main idea is that those who affect the library's future must understand that the library constituency is paying attention and will speak out on behalf of libraries. Trustees can and should make it extremely difficult for your library to suffer from benign neglect or worse at the hands of campus or city governors.

CREATE AN ADVISORY BOARD

If you are in a library that does not have such an elected or appointed board but reports directly to a higher-level administrator, then you would be wise to develop your own "advisory" board. This board, separate from the Friends group (which is discussed in the next section), should be a board comprised of "heavy hitters." It could be developed as a foundation board for resource development, with the added responsibility that this board advises you on matters of library services and promotion, or it could simply be an advisory board. If you are trying to assemble such a group from scratch, make contact with a person you know within your community (be it campus, city, or corporate) who has some political connections and who has expressed support for the library—one of your influential patrons, perhaps.

Working with at least one person of influence outside the library, you can come up with a list of potential board members. If you are not structurally set with a board, this process could actually be a rare opportunity to enlist a powerful group of supporters to the library's cause. A little research should enable you to determine the steps necessary to institutionalize such a group. It is unlikely that you'll be stopped from trying to formalize a "library advisory board" that has the ostensive purpose of giving input into service direction but which can actually become advocates.

If it is too difficult to make such a structural change within your larger organization, and if you don't already have a Friends group, you could certainly develop your own Friends organization. If starting from scratch, you have an opportunity to make sure that you get influential members on board. Let them know that you are seeking not only advice and fund-raising support, but that the library needs their active political support as well, to ensure that the library gets the resources and policies it needs to continue to be successful and relevant into the future.

FRIENDS GROUPS

Friends groups come in all sizes and with all kinds of agendas. Very often Friends groups are organized to raise funds and give monetary support to the library. It is quite likely that they are involved in some aspect of library programming and even library promotion. Whatever the traditional mission, becoming *the* grassroots support group for the library should move to the top of their agenda. Friends groups can raise more money with one effective campaign that promotes a new building than with hundreds of used-book sales. With a lot less time and effort (and a lot more satisfaction) your Friends group is just the group to organize a targeted campaign for your library.

Friends groups are typically structured as 501© 3 organizations. While this special status allows them to operate exempt from taxation, it does limit how much money they can spend on campaigns. With ingenuity, energy, and commitment, however, the money needed for a campaign can fall well within legal limits. What they've got that money can't buy is members! Hopefully, lots and lots of members. They can work with their membership to get the word out about what the library needs and how the membership can help. In addition, they can leverage that membership by establishing an "each one reach one" campaign.

Your Friends group need not be comprised of the community's movers and shakers (although that certainly doesn't hurt). With a well-thought-out campaign to get the library's message out, the sheer numbers of your Friends group (along with all the people in their sphere of influence) will have a strong effect on your organization's leadership.

The Friends group for your organization has power. They may not know it yet and they may not have used it, but they do represent the stakeholders of your campus or community. And they're organized around a cause they believe in—the library. That's some rich starting ground. The Friends can and should be encouraged to help you get the library's message out on an ongoing basis. And particularly for a targeted campaign, they will be invaluable for support (see Part III).

If you haven't discussed advocacy with your Friends, now is the time to do so. If getting into the world of political promotion is new to your Friends, you would be wise to bring them along from the very beginning. Use your Friends organization for focus groups. Involve your Friends in developing the message. As members of the "laity," they will undoubtedly have great perspective on what "sells." What sounds important and powerful to us may not sound so to people who have lives beyond the library. Many members of the Friends group may have expertise in areas that can help you craft and then deliver the message. Marketing techniques from the business world are usually transferable and the business world has been involved in garnering support for products and services for a long time. Most important, by involving your key support group in the development of your message, you will go a long way in ensuring they take the lead in delivering it.

DEVELOP A FRIENDS GROUP

If you don't have a Friends group, develop one now. Even if you are ready to embark on a campaign it's not too late. In fact, having a targeted need may help you get people interested and involved more readily. Developing a Friends group shouldn't be that difficult. You know who your friends are already—they are the people who use your library and have expressed their support for the library on an informal basis. Talk to some of your most loyal and outspoken patrons. See if you can get a small group of them together for a meeting to discuss the possibility of them forming, or helping you to form, a Friends group. Contact some lead members of neighboring Friends organizations and see if they would provide information and assistance in the development of a Friends organization for your library.

Because nothing will be as powerful as having a self-selected library support group when working to make the case for your library, it is important that the fledgling Friends group aim to amass a large membership. Obviously, the group will need operating funds, so a membership fee is important; however, you may want to strongly consider making membership as inexpensive as possible so that you get as many joiners as possible. In the end, a large Friends coffer will not net the library as much as hundreds of stakeholders working to ensure that the library gets the annual funding it needs to deliver quality services.

Once you have brought together a core committee to establish a Friends group and have received advice and guidance from another Friends group or from the state library, you need to begin the membership drive. Many libraries prohibit using the library's patron list for anything other than direct library purposes—it may be that you are not comfortable stretching "library purposes" to cover the Friends. There are, however, other ways to generate membership.

Because patrons are obvious choices for membership, you can work with the new Friends committee to develop a membership form to distribute to every patron at the circulation desk. For a public library, a clip-and-send ad in the local newspaper can generate significant results. The price will be fairly high in most cases, but you are likely to find a way to get a donation from a local business or leader to fund it. It will be money well spent.

If you do not encounter objection from the administration, parents can make good targets for a Friends membership drive in an academic setting. Let your administration know that a Friends group can help promote the library and support special programming. In addition, target the alumni association because they, too, will be likely supporters of the library. Be sure that you have decided ahead of time what your objective is for Friends. If, ultimately, you want to have a strong mailing list for advocacy activities, you will want to keep the cost for joining fairly low—with options for increased financial support.

Certainly you will want to have incentives for joining the Friends. As you are getting started, it's important not to be overly ambitious in what you can offer members. Promising to put them on the preferred mailing list for the library's newsletter and promotional materials may be sufficient. In time, a growing and thriving Friends group will begin to engage in fund-raising activities and programs, and this will offer additional opportunities for giving preference to Friends members and thereby increasing membership.

Developing a Friends group isn't really all that difficult. Most libraries have been working with Friends groups for years. In fact, if you identify the libraries you know who are successful in getting the funding they need and the libraries that are regarded as important by their larger organizations, you will undoubtedly find that these libraries have strong and active Friends groups as well.

It may take some time and initial arm twisting to get a Friends group up and running but this grassroots organization is usually critical to a library's ability to get the support it needs from those who have ultimate say over a library's budget. In addition, as policy issues arise on the state, national, or local level, you will need to have an identifiable group of library supporters to wage the kind of public opinion campaign that is needed to influence legislation.

Without a Friends group, you will be working to coalesce a support group each time you wish to influence funding or policy for libraries. With a Friends group, you always have a politically powerful group at the ready. A Friends group, by its very existence, communicates that libraries are important to the community's stakeholders and that your library is important enough that supporters volunteer their time, money, and effort to ensuring that the library gets what it needs to be successful.

BACK TO YOU

As mentioned earlier, the fact that you are reading this book means that you are interested in what it takes to make a good strong case for your library. In truth, being an effective advocate takes hard work and courage. Hard work because big change rarely comes quickly or easily; courage because speaking out may not come naturally and may not be appreciated by those who have hired you and can, just as easily, fire you.

While a good message and a great cadre of supporters are critical, tenacity is often what finally wins out. However, if you're not prepared to outlast the administrators, funders, and policy makers you may win a small battle but you will not, in all likelihood, establish the library as an important priority for funding long-term. I sometimes think of advocacy as akin to water torture. It's the steady drip, drip, drip that finally wins out. Unless your library is already fully funded and you are respected as the resident expert for all information policy within your larger organization, don't think of advocacy as a one-time effort. Advocacy will succeed on a one-time basis if you only have a one-time need. If you are typical, however, you are constantly fighting the battle for better funding. Policy issues are always evolving, and they may evolve away from such critical issues as equality of access and intellectual freedom if you are not always paying attention and getting the message out about the importance of library services.

Advocacy takes courage; you cannot create fundamental change without taking risks. Some of those risks are intensely personal. Many library directors are at-will employees who have little protection from disgruntled administrators. It is my personal and strong belief, however, that being an effective advocate is a critical component of the director's job. If a director is unwilling to take the risk of getting the word out about what it will take to deliver services, if that director is uncomfortable generating strong political support for the library, then that director should seriously consider whether he or she is in the right job. In most cases, if the director is unwilling to commit to a strong advocacy campaign, it just won't happen and the ones who will suffer from that in the end are the very patrons we are hired to serve.

The good news is that we can mitigate the risk to a significant extent by being smart about our efforts. Not only will the library's message be strengthened by the support of Friends and trustees, but these groups can insulate you from the front line of battle. It is very important that, while you empower your support groups to work on advocacy, you are seen by the powers that be as the library's main cheerleader and lead spokesperson. This is not to say that you can abdicate the responsibility for making the case to others—in all likelihood it won't happen (or won't happen well) without you.

To be effective, you must be willing to communicate strongly and effectively with your boss about what it will take to deliver services and what the consequences will be to the larger organization if you are not successful. Sometimes that means taking a strong stand and telling unwelcome truths. Sometimes it does take courage but if you are respectful, you can also be direct. Amazingly, by taking a stand, being honest and forthright, and by doing it all in a strong and respectful manner, you may well elevate your status in the eyes of your administration and government.

PART II

DELIVERING THE MESSAGE

3 CREATING THE CONTINUOUS CAMPAIGN

A successful ongoing library campaign creates a base of support that can be moved to action for a targeted campaign in the future, is present in all your library promotions, and makes successful use of all forms of media.

Avenues for getting the word out about your library include:

- Newsletters
- Letters to the editor and op-ed pieces
- Television coverage
- Public service announcements
- General promotional materials
- Annual reports
- Endorsements
- Presentations

Libraries everywhere have become increasingly sophisticated in getting the word out about their library services. Borrowing heavily from business marketing techniques, libraries use everything from bookmarks, to program brochures, to newsletters, to annual reports to let their communities know what they have to offer and how well they are doing at delivering their services. Too often, however, libraries tout their services but fail to let the public and their communities know *why what the library has to offer matters.*

Luckily, if you are doing a good job at promoting your library, your work is almost done. You are just one short step away from turning good public relations material into excellent political material that both promotes and advocates. This chapter shows how libraries can make their standard promotional materials achieve high impact politically—how adding a few words can show both users and nonusers not only the vast array of services available from the library, but why those services make a difference in the lives of individuals and in the health of the community, school, or campus.

Libraries have huge popularity ratings. I think one would be hard pressed to find anyone who would staunchly support the demise of libraries. How then to explain the constant uphill battle libraries fight every day and every year to ensure adequate funding? How do we explain our "invisibility" to the leaders of our organizations? Why must we fight so hard to gain a voice in setting public and organizational policy (let alone the lead voice when that policy involves access to information and determination of goals for literacy and learning)?

I think it's because we fail to show how critical libraries are to the success of our larger communities. Many leaders do not use libraries even if they have "fond" memories of their childhood library experiences. I believe we suffer from the "Mom and Apple Pie" sentiment that supports a belief by many that libraries will always be around and require no special, let alone political, support. People like libraries—that means we've done a good job of promoting and providing services. People don't tend to fight for libraries, however, unless the library is in a crisis situation—that means we have not shared with our public why libraries are essential and what it takes to keep them relevant.

The good news is that we already have the tools to make a powerful case for the library. The final step is to use those tools to generate support for the library on an ongoing basis and to use those tools (and the support we've generated) to ensure that our targeted campaigns for funding, building, and policy are overwhelmingly supported.

Chapter 1 discussed developing a politically strong message. The ongoing campaign should be designed to send that message every day, in using all your avenues of promotion and communication. Waging a successful ongoing campaign can be as easy as making a mental shift in the way you present yourself to your public.

In all likelihood, you are already engaged in promoting your library and its services using a variety of techniques. Bookmarks, newsletters, press releases, flyers, program brochures, and speaking engagements are all typical ways in which we communicate our services to our patrons and potential patrons. Ensuring that everything you say and publish using these methods includes your message is a simple but important step.

The sections that follow show you how to deliver your message effectively about the importance of your library.

NEWSLETTERS

The power of the press. That's what you have at your disposal if your library publishes a newsletter. Certainly a newsletter is an important and effective way to let your patrons and supporters know what's happening at the library. If you are not also using this tool to let them know why what you're providing *matters* then you are losing half the value of the publication. It's great if your library is offering preschool story times, but why stop at letting folks know when they are taking place? Why not include a front-page story on literacy and how the best and cheapest way to ensure that all adults can read is to catch them early—to introduce children to a books and learning environment early on so that they don't become adults who can't read. What are the statistics on illiteracy in your community? How do library story times generate models for parents and make reading a fundamental activity in the family?

Whether or not your newsletter readers have children, they do care about literacy rates. For example, does your audience know that nearly 80 percent of America's prisoners are functionally illiterate? Do they know that according to the National Center on Institutions and Alternatives it costs an average of over $20,000 per year to house a single prisoner? Literacy matters to everyone and libraries are incredible bargains—especially when you consider the alternatives. Make what you are doing meaningful to your entire audience (the parents who want to know when to bring their kids in for story time constitute the choir). Here is an opportunity to show why what you are doing makes a difference to the larger organization. Powerful.

Think about this tactic every time you publish your newsletter. Commit to ensuring that each issue has a brief article on why the events and information within the newsletter matters. If your academic library publishes a newsletter to announce important new acquisitions, be sure to include a paragraph or two on why those acquisitions matter. How is your collection helping the institution achieve its goals? How is collection development important to the academic success of students? How do your services support continuing research by faculty?

It's not enough just to report what your library has and what you are doing. It's not enough to let your readers know about new programs and materials. Every issue and every article should also be reporting on why it matters. Often, a leading sentence will do the trick. "In response to increasing evidence that teens need productive and exciting ways to spend their time after school, the Anytown Public Library announces Teens Online, an after-school Internet program especially for kids aged 13–16." Now you've not only said "what" but why it matters.

Figures 3.1–3.10 are examples of newsletter articles that make the case as well as provide information about programs and services. In these figures and throughout the rest of the book, I have underscored key passages that present a strong message.

NPL Newsletter

NORFOLK PUBLIC LIBRARY

www.npl.lib.va.us

April/May 1999

Read! Learn! Connect! @ the Library!
Celebrate National Library Week, April 11-17

April 11-17, 1999

Join us to celebrate National Library Week with special storyhours, school-age, teen, and family programs.

Volume III, Number 4
April/May 1999

This newsletter is published by The Friends of the Norfolk Public Library. To make suggestions about topics or articles please call 664-7338.

Today's libraries are more vital than ever. Most of us could never afford to buy the books, magazines, videos, CD-ROMs, and more the library offers our families. In addition to books and print resources, the Norfolk Public Library offers access to computers and the Internet that most residents don't have at home.

This year's National Library Week, April 11-17, celebrates the freedom to "Read! Learn! Connect! @ the Library" - a freedom easily taken for granted. Libraries are an American value, born of the notion that a free people should have free access to information. In practice what that means is that libraries give us access to a full spectrum of information and ideas that allow us to learn what we want, explore many points of view and make informed decisions.

More than 200 years after Benjamin Franklin introduced the first lending library, it's easy to take for granted one of

our basic freedoms - the freedom to explore the whole world of ideas and information at your local library. In 1953, President Eisenhower wrote a statement that is just as relevant today. "The libraries of America are and must ever remain the home of free, inquiring minds. To them, our citizens...must be able to turn with clear confidence that there they can freely seek the whole truth."

As we race headlong into a technological age that is sure to surprise in ways we can't even imagine, it's important to remember Eisenhower's words. Libraries will remain the solid foundation from which information will flow. But only if we, the citizens who use and benefit from libraries, support them as the keepers of our freedom to read, learn, and connect.

Be sure to visit your library during National Library Week and throughout the year. See the insert in this newsletter for a listing of free programs.

Figure 3.1—Norfolk (Va.) Public Library newsletter.

This newsletter shows the value of libraries—they are economical and they are important for intellectual freedom.

Director's Message

As the 16th Director for America's third largest public research library, our leadership focuses on Cleveland Public Library as **"The People's University: Striving for Excellence."** Thus, we are building upon the good legacies of past directors and a great library history that created this premier library system to propel us into the next century.

Launching *Speaking Volumes* as our first community newsletter reflects a personal belief in a critical need to create and nurture a renewed community interest in library news and events. As information is power, your library will use this communication instrument to empower 'the people' with additional knowledge about their major citywide information resource—The People's University.

We always recognize three significant factors that I believe contributed to the success of Cleveland Public Library for over 130 years:
a) a reputable collection of informational materials, b) a trained staff of professionals to provide library service, and c) very strong support from our community. Our leadership will meet the new challenges and ensure that the standards of measurement that created this premier library system are rigorously maintained.

As the 'new university' in our community, the neutrality of our mission requires us to serve the informational interests and needs of all citizens. Our lifelong learning curriculum is ably delivered every day by 600 professional library ambassadors who will welcome you with courtesy and connect you to the worldwide information you are seeking.

Andrew Venable

Andrew A. Venable, Jr., Director
Cleveland Public Library

"PRESERVE OUR FUTURE, SUPPORT THE PEOPLE'S UNIVERSITY"

Children's Services Takes New Turns

Programs and services for children at the Cleveland Public Library (CPL) are taking new turns with the renovation of the Main Library and the addition of grants, funded projects, and programs. The mosaic globe designed by local artists and children at library branches was funded by the Eaton Corporation and accomplished with the assistance of the Committee for Public Art. The Eaton Foundation gave additional funds to create an inviting entryway to the department and to purchase additional toys and books.

Partnerships with community agencies mark the work of the Children's Services staff. In September many tours and school visits to our branches and the Main Library, and presentations to high school and elementary classes by visiting authors, Jacqueline Woodson and Pat Cummings, took place. Summer and Winter Reading Clubs encourage children to read for fun and to maintain reading skills. Partners for these programs have been the Cleveland Browns, Cleveland Metroparks Zoo, Cleveland Cavaliers, the Friends of the Library, and many local agencies who donated prizes for weekly drawings. This fall, the Playhouse Square Children's Theater series collaborated with the Main Library Children's Literature Department to offer a schedule of joint programs for families.

Forming community partnerships has also been a goal of The Family Learning Connection Project, begun by CPL two years ago to provide family-oriented programs and services and access to computer technology. This year, due to a major grant from the Carnegie Corporation of New York, the Project will begin an Early Childhood Literacy Initiative. The Initiative will attempt to fill the need for emergent literacy support for young children (infants to age five) by establishing an outreach program to child care centers in Cleveland, create early childhood learning environments in 15 branch

A phenomenally successful library card sign-up campaign, co-sponsored by Cleveland Public Library and Cleveland Municipal School District, resulted in 16,039 students, more than 20% of the district, registering.

libraries, and offer training sessions for CPL's Children's Librarians and general public through an "Early Childhood Institute." The Parent Child Workshop, a five-week series of programs for children with parent or caregiver, will also be presented at many branches as part of the Initiative.

Through this project, CPL will dramatically further its role as a community partner in creating literate families. Children will enter school better equipped with reading readiness skill. Cleveland Public Library hopes to build on a century of service to children with a wide array of programs and services for children and families.

They Spoke Volumes
Arnold H. Glasow
"The fewer the facts, the stronger the opinion."

Figure 3.2—Cleveland (Ohio) Public Library newsletter.

The director's message portrays the public library as the "People's University," elevating its importance in the reader's mind.

Chestatee Regional Library System
127 Main Street, NW
Gainesville, GA 30505-2399

Address Correction Requested

DIRECTIONS

by Diane Bronson, Library Director

How have libraries changed your life?
Now that's a question. Many of us are ardent library users and can't remember a time when the library wasn't important to us. Others may find the library occasionally useful, or a delightful pastime. But for how many of us has it changed our lives?

The essay that follows was given to me by another library director, who received it from a patron during National Library Week in response to that question. It says a lot about why libraries exist and why we who work for them feel so good and so strongly about what we do. I hope you enjoy reading it as much as I did!

I had such a nomadic childhood. My father was a security guard for the British Embassy, and we were always on the move. Sometimes we were lucky enough to be in a foreign country as long as three years, but it could vary anywhere from 6 months on up.

As you can well imagine my formal schooling was uneven at best with some periods where I didn't go to school at all. The six months that we were in Warsaw, Poland my parents just couldn't afford the fees for the local English speaking school.

Everywhere we went there always seemed to be a library of some sort. Even if it was only a small limited library in the British Embassy. Most of the time you just helped yourself. There was no one to guide me and I just picked books that looked interesting. So I was reading Charles Dickens by the age of nine. Sometimes I was lucky enough to find a large English public library, then I was in heaven! Books became my dearest friends in a sometimes lonely childhood. My father was always complaining, "Carole's always got her nose in a book"!

My fondest fantasy as a child was that I would accidentally get locked in a library over night, and could browse to my heart's content.

When I was thirteen, and my brother was born, my mother decided she needed me at home to help her. That was the end of my formal education as I never did return to school. But thanks to libraries I have never stopped learning. I have learned to speak correct English, how to act in most situations. In fact, I would say that most of everything I know came from between the pages of a book. When I've been sad they've cheered me up, when I've needed reminding of my blessings I can read about others' challenges.

Thanks to books I recently sat for my GED at the age of 50, and excuse me for bragging, but I got some pretty high scores. Not bad for someone who left school at 13!

Yes, I can honestly say some of my best friends are books, and one of my favorite places to be is the library. My advice to anyone who reads this is please turn off the TV, come to your local library, and "get your nose in a book"!

Figure 3.3—Chestatee Regional Library System newsletter, Dahlonega, Ga.

The director of this library tells stories to show how libraries change lives.

ELA AREA PUBLIC LIBRARY

Footnotes

Volume 12, Issue 1   Fall 1999

From the Director

"What's happening with the new library building project?" That's the first question everyone asks me when we meet. Now, with architects chosen and a few target dates to shoot for, we are ready to embark on our own "2001: A More Space Odyssey."

At the end of the ride, sometime in the year 2001, we'll have a library almost twice as large as this one with more of the materials, programs and services you've told us you want.

In July, after interviewing several firms, your library trustees selected Sente & Rubel, Ltd., Architects of Northbrook to design the new library. Some of their local projects include the Grayslake Public Library and the Ela Area YMCA. Their design philosophy emphasizes making sure that the building and grounds will enhance the surrounding community.

The first leg of the journey, planning and design, will take about nine months; then construction will begin. The ground-breaking is tentatively set for late spring of 2000, and we plan to "land" at our new location by early fall of 2001.

Yes, it may seem like a long trip, but we are determined to have a library that everyone in the entire district can be proud of!

Watch future *Footnotes*, our home page, displays and handouts as well as the local newspapers for progress reports. As always, feel free to call or e-mail me with your questions.
                                        Carol Larson, Director

Explore the World Through Your Library!

Your Ela Area Public Library card brings you so much! It entitles you to the latest books and other materials for entertainment or research. With the help of our staff and Internet terminals, you can visit virtually any place in the world and get the information you need. You can also join in our innovative programs for all ages. If you are new to the district, or if you live here but don't have a current card, come in and get one during September - National Library Card Signup Month! You'll get a free canvas tote bag (one per family) to help you carry all the exciting materials you're going to find, and a brochure on how to manage your account.

As the world of choices explodes, librarians are increasingly needed for help in navigating the vast range of resources. At the same time, patrons have shown they want to be more self-sufficient about managing their library usage. Some of the programs we offer this fall will make it easier for you to get the information you want. The do-it-yourself workshop shows you how to avoid lines at Checkout and look up your own records in private, keep track of items on your card and access online subscriptions from your home. Our new Homework Center will open Oct 4. Ever-popular book discussion groups and make-it-yourself craft classes are back. We also offer Internet classes and individual tutoring sessions to help you navigate the Web. See our latest list of family-friendly resources (p. 5)!

There are so many ways to get involved with your library this fall!
● Join the Friends this month during their annual membership drive (p. 7);
● Take the family to the Ela Festival of Arts and enjoy our poetry program (p. 5);
● Visit our Tradition & Technology display at the Lake County Museum and help us gather photos for the local history collection (p. 3);
● Check out Teen Read Week Oct. 17-23 (p. 3);
● Speak out at the Community Forum on Nov. 6 (p. 5);
● Sign up for the Children's Book Week raffle (p. 4);
● Come hear renowned read-aloud advocate Jim Trelease (p. 3) and authors of children's books, thrillers, local geology studies and art history.

So come to the programs, make the crafts, enjoy the classes, and - as always - check out what you need. Explore your library!

Figure 3.4—Ela Area Public Library newsletter, Lake Zurich, Ill.

This newsletter highlights the importance of *librarians* in the new information age.

ELA AREA PUBLIC LIBRARY

Footnotes

Volume 11, Issue 3   Spring 1999

From the Director's Desk

Two years ago, realizing that the building and associated parking would soon be inadequate for future needs, your library trustees began long range planning to address the challenges of ongoing growth within the district.

They gathered extensive input from residents with a telephone survey, a direct mail survey and 20 focus groups.

Responses showed several recurring priorities, including your desire to have more materials and parking. Feedback was very favorable for a larger building if it could stay in the same vicinity.

Working with a space planning consultant and an architect, trustees determined that a 60,000 sq. ft. building and 200 parking spaces were needed to serve a district of our projected size. When land behind the library became available recently, the board purchased it.

To build will require a $13.9 million bond issue, translating to $30 for a $150,000 home or $41 for a $200,000 home.

Please read the letter on page 5 and attend a public meeting here either Tues., Mar. 2 or Wed., Mar. 3 at 7pm so we can give you more details and answer your questions. You are also welcome to attend the board's next meeting, Mar. 16 at 6pm. Join us!

Carol Larson, Director

Attracting Patrons of All Kinds

In a recent Gallup poll measuring public opinion on libraries, 90% of respondents across all age groups said that, regardless of increased technology, libraries will continue to be needed in the future. This view may prevail partly because an overwhelming majority (65%) of respondents typically consulted librarians on their visits, and almost that many (50%) enjoyed reading newspapers or magazines within the comfortable atmosphere of the library.

Americans visit libraries three times as often as they go to the movies. What keeps them coming back, according to a study by the Benton Foundation, is the "value added" by the librarians and support staff who guide patrons' research, help them find that perfect mystery to read, or introduce the guest performer for the day's free program. Most respondents remembered going to the library as children and, whether empty-nesters or young singles, they regularly returned for that same connection.

One morning, we asked some of our patrons why they visited us. Ernest Paul, 51, came in for reference help while Ada Toniolo, also 51, came in to pick up some tax forms. Susan Tracy, 35, wanted to do research with reference help nearby. "Whenever a problem arises in my life," she told us, "I go to the library and read 5 or 10 books on the subject. This has been a tremendous help!"

Dorothy Noble, age 73, wanted to greet friends and get materials for leisure reading. She also came to look for some feature videos, which she wishes she could reserve! Audiovisual materials are becoming very popular for patrons such as Sharlene Szostek, 34. "I come in every Monday for CDs for my workouts. *(cont. on p. 6)*

Daily visits from a deer we called Dewey brightened our winter months.

Figure 3.5—Ela Area Public Library newsletter, Lake Zurich, Ill.

The author uses the fact that an overwhelming number of Americans value libraries and librarians as an endorsement of the importance and popularity of libraries.

December 1997

Cool Café Teens Present Haunt Night at Kirn

Ghosts and haunts and howling bones were on the scene in the Kirkby Room of Kirn Memorial Library the evening of October 28. *Haunt Night* was presented by nine young men who are participants in the Cool Café evening teen group.

The program included a tour of the "Library Morgue," snacks, videos and staged performances of three ghost stories. Lighted Jack-o-lanterns, ghostly sounds and Halloween fun were on hand for the 50 or more people who came to experience *Haunt Night*.

Children ages 10 and older were invited through flyers distributed

by the Cool Café teens, signs in all the branches and an event listing in the local newspaper.

For the participants of Cool Café, *Haunt Night* was the culmination of many nights of reading, planning, practicing and having a great time with friends. Cool Café is open to teens ages 13 to 18 and meets every Thursday at 5:00 p.m. at Kirn Memorial Library in downtown Norfolk.

Cool Café is a couple hours of booktalking, brainstorming, eating and hanging out with some superactive teens with great potential who just happen to know how to have a great time. *Haunt Night* was the first of what we hope will be many Cool Café ventures.

by Linda Braddock

Issue Number 20
December 1997

http://www.whro.org/cl/npl

This newsletter is published monthly by The Friends of the Norfolk Public Library. To make suggestions about topics or articles please call 664-7338.

From the Director's Office: The Future is Here

Kids who read succeed. The Norfolk Public Library is committed to ensuring that all of our children develop a love of reading because we know that a reading habit started early pays off for life. But a reading habit must be nourished all along the way and that's why we are sharpening our focus on teens.

Adolescence is a turbulent and exciting time. While teens are pushing boundaries we want to be sure that they are also stretching their minds and imaginations. Books can take teens anywhere they want to go -- from fantasy to far away places,

to finding solutions and support for their special concerns.

As we build new services and programs for teens, we are getting advice and assistance from experts -- teens themselves. Thanks to our Teen Advisory Board we have been able to develop a teen reading-discussion series, host a haunted house, and even design a new teen center which will soon take shape on Kirn Library's second floor.

The future is here, the future is our youth. We welcome them.

Sally G. Reed, Director

Figure 3.6—Norfolk (Va.) Public Library newsletter.

Connecting the importance of libraries and literacy for teens—a traditionally hard to reach group and an important age for developing and retaining a love of reading.

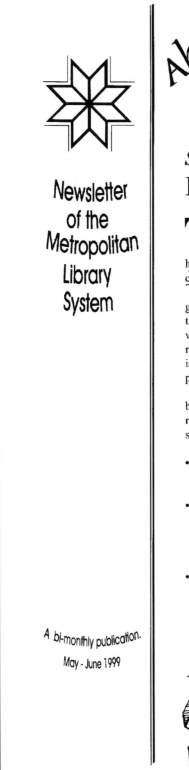

About Your Libraries

Newsletter
of the
Metropolitan
Library
System

A bi-monthly publication.

May - June 1999

Summer Reading
Building a Community of Readers

The library system's 1999 Summer Reading Program will encourage a love for books and reading as it helps hone the reading skills of our children.

Thousands of preschoolers and grade school children are expected to participate between June 1 and July 31. Each will set a reading goal and win prizes for reaching it. Special events in the libraries will enhance the summer reading experience.

Co-sponsoring the program, the library system's largest and most far-reaching, are the following community-spirited businesses and organizations.

- **Sonic**, a valued sponsor for three years, is giving each summer reader a book bag.
- **The Oklahoma Redhawks** will host "Library Night at the Ballpark" in early August. Summer readers who reach their reading goal will receive two free tickets to the game.
- **The National Cowboy Hall of Fame** will salute summer reading's western theme—Yippee Yi Yo! Join the Read Stampede—by giving each participant a free admission to the Hall.
- **Oklahoma Children's Theatre** has a great gift: one free ticket for each summer reading finisher.
- Wonderful **KMGL Magic 104 Radio**, a supporter of practically every library system endeavor for more than a decade, will spread the good word about the summer reading program and encourage kids to join, read and win.
- Ditto for the **Daily Oklahoman**, which has been a summer reading supporter for years.
- And, last but certainly not least, the **Oklahoma Department of Libraries** supports libraries throughout the state by printing summer reading promotional posters, bookmarks and reading logs for the children and by providing assistance to the librarians who share the library daily with our children.

Figure 3.7—Metropolitan Library System newsletter, Oklahoma City, Okla.

This library has taken the opportunity to introduce the summer reading program by first stating why it matters.

Volume II, Number 6
June 1998

This newsletter is published 10 times per year by The Friends of the Norfolk Public Library. To make suggestions about topics or articles please call 664-7338.

Thank You

Many of the Norfolk Public Library's programs and services are supported by generous donations from our community. The Library recognizes the following for their generous support:

The Town Foundation has donated several new computers, printers and furniture for the Barron F. Black Homework Learning Center. The much needed equipment will help meet the demand for computer services at this location.

Newsletter

NORFOLK PUBLIC LIBRARY
www.npl.lib.va.us

June 1998

From the Director's Office:
Working to Create a City of Readers

There may be no other issue facing our city and our nation as important as literacy. As we head into the 21st century it is becoming increasingly clear that in order to be employed and live productively, people will need to be literate -- both in the traditional sense, as well as being technologically literate. Jobs that depend on nothing more than manual labor, once plentiful in the agricultural and industrial eras, are becoming more complex and are beginning to require basic levels of literacy and computer competency. The byproduct of our failure to ensure that everyone is literate is clear and costly -- it is estimated, for example, that nearly 80% of America's prisoners are functionally illiterate.

The Norfolk Public Library recognizes the important role we play in the prevention of illiteracy at the earliest ages and the role we play supporting literacy and learning at all ages. In an important and visionary move, citizens and agencies across our city are banding together to raise the profile on literacy and to work together to ensure that everyone in Norfolk can read. This literacy collective, being led by Norfolk Public Schools, includes a broad base of representation from city and community agencies, individuals, businesses and corporations who have a vested interest in working to improve literacy. The Norfolk Public Library is pleased to be a part of this initiative.

Schools cannot solve the problem of illiteracy alone. An individual's chance to be both literate and successful begins at birth. Parents must understand and appreciate that from day one a child is learning about language and how it is used. The Norfolk Public Library has a variety of programs, services and materials to encourage and help parents begin reading to their newborns and toddlers. Literacy is a life-time skill and our mission is to provide support for life-long learning. Our mission is to "Create a City of Readers."

Sally G. Reed, Director

Figure 3.8—Norfolk (Va.) Public Library newsletter.

Here libraries are shown as partners in preventing illiteracy.

About Tall Tree:

The Reader's Digest Foundation Tall Tree Initiative for Library Services is dedicated to the creation of a new model for children's library service in Westchester County, based on full collaboration between public libraries and local schools. The Tall Tree Initiative is demonstrating how educators and librarians can work together to prepare our children for the 21st century.

GOALS of the Tall Tree Initiative

To enable children to become better and more enthusiastic readers, with the ability to read not just for information, but as a source of enjoyment and personal enrichment.

To help children develop the strong basic academic skills and abilities to become competitive 21st century citizens.

To allow children to become competent and confident creators and users of information, in many formats, knowing how to seek, evaluate and apply their skills to a variety of problems and situations.

By working together, schools and libraries can enhance students' information skills and experiences far beyond what each institution could provide individually. Tall Tree success can already be seen at the New Rochelle Public Library and nearby Daniel Webster School, the project's first joint site. Peekskill's Field Library and Peekskill City Schools are currently engaged in the second Tall Tree venture, while mini-grants, seminars and other programs are spreading the Tall Tree message to communities throughout Westchester.

Since creating the Tall Tree Initiative in 1995, the Reader's Digest Foundation has provided nearly $3 million in grants to support and expand it countywide. Like a tall tree transforming the landscape, Tall Tree's collaborative vision is transforming Westchester's education scene.

Tall Tree News

Winter 2000 · Volume 3 · Issue 1

Dual Language Learning on the Rise

Dual language programs, also referred to as bilingual education, enable students to develop proficiency in English and in another language by receiving instruction in both. Spanish is the most common target language. In a Spanish two-way program, students in both language groups get ample exposure to both Spanish and English. In this way, they can progress academically in both languages simultaneously. These programs are flexible enough so that communities can tailor them to local demographics and culture.

Research reveals that the dual language approach is effective not only in teaching both languages to students in two different language groups, but also in developing students' overall academic excellence. Schools with dual language programs demonstrate student achievement on many standardized tests as students show academic progress and fluency in both languages. In a 1994 study by Collier, five urban districts showed that language minority students (Hispanic in this instance) in two-way

continued on back page

On-Site in Peekskill: Books Come Alive

Tall Tree programs have bloomed throughout Peekskill, reaching out from The Woodside School to all the elementary schools: Hillcrest, Oakside, and Uriah Hill. To kick off the **Books Come Alive** program, reading specialist **Dr. Lindamichelle-baron** (sic) conducted an interactive workshop at The Paramount Center for the Arts for first and second grade teachers throughout the district, reading specialists, other educators, and the Field Library Children's Room staff. **Wit, Wisdom, and Words** was, in the words of one teacher, "a fabulous, inspiring workshop! Now I realize how important it is to inject the school day with 'fun' language."

Also at the Paramount Center in November was a presentation of **A Very Hungry Caterpillar** based on the book by **Eric Carle**. 875 students from Oakside and Uriah Hill in grades K-2 attended along with 50 teachers and 20 staff. And in November there was a Theater Works presentation of the **Three Little Pigs** at the Oakside School Cafetorium for 900 students in grades K-2.

Illustrator **Yumi Heo** visited Peekskill in November and environmental singer and storyteller **Linda Richards** visited in December, each giving morning presentations at the Oakside School and afternoon presentations at the

continued on page 5

Figure 3.9—Tall Tree newsletter, Ardsley, N.Y.

This newsletter shows libraries as partner in bilingual education support, which is highly valued by the community.

SOUTHWEST
PUBLIC LIBRARIES
OF FRANKLIN COUNTY

EXTRA! EXTRA! EXTRA!
Read All About It

| Vol. 1, No. 1. | News from Southwest Public Libraries | April, 1999 |

National Library Week April 11-17, 1999

We're Celebrating the Freedom to Read

This year's National Library Week, April 11-17, celebrates the freedom to "Read! Learn! Connect! at the Library" that has helped make our nation great.

"There's something for everyone at the library," said Frances Black, Director of Southwest Public Libraries. "Today, more than ever, libraries provide a variety of resources that help people of all ages connect with the information they need for school, work or personal fulfillment. All you need is a library card."

At Southwest Public Libraries these resources include access to more than 2 million books, videos and recordings via Discovery Place (online catalog), the Internet, via The Library Channel, free programs for children and adults, OPLIN (Ohio Public Information Network), Infotrac (online periodicals) and much more. **Check it out today!**

Mayor Grossman Proclaims "Library Week" in Grove City

Cheryl Grossman, Mayor of Grove City is proclaiming that the week of April 11-17 is "Library Week" in Grove City. Grossman is to present a proclamation during the week to Library Director Frances Black making it official.

The official proclamation reads:

Whereas, our nation's public libraries provide all people with books, computers, videocassettes, audio tapes and other resources to enrich their lives:

Whereas, librarians protect the right of all Americans to read, learn and connect to information representing all points of view;

Whereas, libraries are vital to building a nation of readers and creating a lifelong love of reading among our children and youth;

Whereas, millions of Americans rely on libraries for their only access to computers and the Internet, allowing them to get connected to our global society;

Whereas, librarians provide the essential support and education needed by children, teenagers and adults alike in their search for knowledge, information and entertainment; and

Whereas, libraries and library supporters nationwide are celebrating National Library Week with the theme "Read! Learn! Connect! at the Library";

Now, therefore, be it resolved that I, Cheryl Grossman, Mayor of Grove City, proclaim April 11-17, 1999, Library Week in Grove City, Ohio and furthermore I encourage all citizens to "Read! Learn! Connect!" by exploring the riches available at our libraries.

"Once you learn to read, you will be forever free."
-- Frederick Douglass

Figure 3.10—Southwest Public Libraries newsletter, Grove City, Ohio.

A mayoral proclamation raises the profile and cache of this library and is displayed prominently on the front page.

If your library is not currently publishing a newsletter, you should seriously consider making that a high priority for your ongoing advocacy campaign. Your Friends group will probably be willing to fund it and send it out to all its members. A newsletter that keeps its allies (the Friends members) aware of larger issues as well as upcoming events helps to cultivate those Friends and makes them educated advocates. Also, an informative newsletter is of significant importance to your patrons, who will be interested in new acquisitions as well as upcoming events. You can give them this important information and educate them about the importance of your services at the same time. When the time comes to prevail upon your patrons and Friends for support in a targeted campaign, they will be much more articulate in supporting the service they value.

In addition to sending the newsletter to Friends members and handing it out at the circulation desk, you should create a VIP mailing list and include all those you wish to influence: your administration, your fellow department heads, business leaders, campus leaders, corporate executives. If you have created a more politically powerful newsletter, then you will be sending them "the message" on a monthly or quarterly basis as well as informing them of all the wonderful things your library is doing.

LETTERS TO THE EDITOR AND "OP-ED" PIECES

Library services are often the solution to problems being reported in the community and campus newspapers. We should not hesitate to use the local newspaper as an avenue to promote the value of libraries. The great thing about the newspaper is its wide readership. While a library newsletter will, primarily, be speaking to the converted, the newspaper reaches a broad audience, many of whom may never have considered the relevance of the library to the issues of the day.

The easiest way to get into print is to write a letter to the editor showing how the library is contributing to the goals and objectives of the community. Positive letters about the library can come from library administration, but they can also come from a trustee or Friend whom you've encouraged to write. In a targeted campaign for a specific issue, letters to the editor can be one component of an aggressive campaign, and in that case, the letters should always come from library supporters rather than from staff.

If you've done a good job in networking and cultivating outsiders to the library's cause, you may well be able to influence one of the paper's own columnists to write an article on the library's behalf. If you don't have connection with the paper and its editorial board, talk to other community leaders whom you've cultivated along the way and see if you can find a connection there. If a particular issue is surfacing in the paper, you may be able simply to call the editorial staff and "pitch" your story to them. Be sure to have a compelling story with all the facts when you call. Although it is often harder to get a staff endorsement of your library that includes the message you want to send, it is usually more effective than a letter to the editor.

National library events such as National Library Week, Teen Read Week, and Banned Books Week are often used successfully by libraries to get local press coverage. Again, it is important when you pitch the idea of coverage to your local newspapers that you make the point, repeatedly, about why it matters. Why do libraries engage in national events? Why is it important to reach out to teens? Why are libraries focusing on banned books? Remember, it often doesn't go without saying so be sure to say it—often—and your chances are excellent that you will see it repeated in print as the columnist or editor's own view.

Figures 3.11, 3.12, and 3.13 are sample letters to the editor and an Op-Ed piece that use persuasion, passion, and facts to make the case and to urge action.

SAMPLE LETTER TO THE EDITOR
[Operating Budget, Public Library]

Dear Editor:

As the chair of the Anytown Public Library I am writing to remind the citizens of this community that the city budget will be developed over the course of the next three months. Now is the time for all citizens who care about their public library to call or write the city administrator and voice support for a 10% increase in the library's operating budget.

10% may seem large but added on a small and inadequate budget up it would translate into only $500,000 extra for the library and would bring our per capita spending on libraries up with the national average. Keeping with the rest of the world is not our goal, however. Providing life-long learning opportunities for every member of this community no matter their background, age, or means is.

Over the last decade the library has been routinely underfunded, especially when compared to the city's overall budget. For example, in the last five years, the city's budget has increased approximately 5% per year. The library, by comparison, has sustained cuts and level funding, and increases for its budget equal only 2% per year. Every year the library falls behind in its ability to bring the citizens of this community access to the latest information technology, an abundance of books for young children just beginning their relationship with books, and hours of operation that meet the needs of a working family.

Here's what an extra $500,000 will mean for all who use the library:

- Sunday hours all year long
- Expanded youth collections at all library locations
- Expanded video collection at the central library
- Internet access for the public at all library locations

Please call your council member and the city administrator at 555-1234. Let them know how important the public library is to you and your family. Let them know that you support a 10% increase for the library's operating budget. We owe it to ourselves; we owe it to our children.

Sincerely yours,

William C. Trustee

Figure 3.11—Sample letter to the editor (operating budget, public library).

In a short letter, funding history is shared along with a clear explication of what additional funding will bring— what's in it for the community.

SAMPLE LETTER TO THE EDITOR

[Operating Budget, Academic Library]

Dear Editor,

If the library is the heart of the campus, then ours needs a triple bypass! As the athletic department continues to grow, our library's hours continue to shrink. As the football team gets new uniforms, our library cuts subscriptions to 20 important research periodicals because they can no longer afford them.

Where are our priorities? Most of us came to this university to learn and to earn a degree – precious few came to enhance their athletic abilities. Yet, that's where the university administrators seem to put all their money.

I don't mean to bash sports—I love football and support the team. I even understand that having a high-profile athletic program helps bring high profile to the university bringing in money (most of which is plowed back into the athletic department). But, hey, here's a thought. Why not focus our revenues on the students? Why not bring high profile to our academic achievement as a recruiting tool?

We can't support high achievement academically without a fully supported library. And guess what . . . if we students get a good education, we might get good jobs. What a great way to build alumni with both the desire and the means to support the university in the long run.

Come on administration. We want longer library hours. We want access to the scholarly journals that support our education. We want librarians available to help with our research. It's time to take a fresh look at our priorities.

Sincerely,

Sue Student

Figure 3.12—Sample letter to the editor (operating budget, academic library).

This letter makes a clear point that academic libraries serve *everyone* and that libraries can be successful recruiting tools for the administration.

Sample Op-Ed Piece

One Percent for Libraries – An Investment in Ourselves

Great cities have great libraries. As Norfolk works to create a "world class city," libraries must not be left behind. Once heralded as a flagship library system in Virginia, the Norfolk Public Library has been in a slow but steady decline over the past decade. Funding, which totaled nearly $4 million and represented 1.2 percent of the city's operating budget in 1987, now stands at less than $3.9 million and equals a mere .79 percent of the city's operating budget.

Good library service costs money – it's as simple as that. But not a lot of money and that's the good news. The Norfolk Public Library Board of Trustees is asking the City Council to appropriate just 1 percent of the city's operating budget to libraries. We think it's one of the best investments they can possibly make to help Norfolk stand out as a city responsive to its citizens' needs and affirms its commitment to education for all people at all stages of life.

As we enter the 21st century, which is already being called "The Information Age," libraries have a key role to play in ensuring that people of all ages and all backgrounds have access to the information and learning resources they need to be productive citizens. Current estimates for the number of illiterate adults in this country range from a low of 10 million to a high of 50 million. The problems that illiteracy creates for our society will only be compounded by the emerging need for citizens to be "techno-literate." Jobs once centering on manual labor are being automated at an extremely high rate. Further, the information our citizens require to meet even the most basic needs is increasingly available in electronic format only.

The city of Norfolk will be especially vulnerable as we move into the new century if it does not focus its attention and resources on education at every level. In 1996, approximately 65 percent of Norfolk's children qualified for the free or reduced lunch program. This indicator of economic distress is also one that often translates into difficulties in school. Children who are economically disadvantaged often do not have the same learning support that other children enjoy, such as home libraries, home computers, opportunities for travel, and parents who were successful themselves in school.

Figure 3.13—Sample Op-Ed piece.

This op-ed piece makes a strong case to connect great libraries (well supported libraries) to the dream for a great city—the goal of city leadership.

The Norfolk Public Library can help close the gap by providing computer acces to information, programs to encourage a life-long habit of reading, and an aggressive outreach program for children "at risk" at the earliest ages so they are prepared and excited to learn when they enter kindergarten. In addition, we must be able to provide an expansive collection that will take the reader to distant places and distant times, as well as provide staff members who are available and well trained to help patrons of all ages find and use the materials they need to be successful in school, in their jobs, and in their daily lives.

The focus our community puts on education must not only encompass traditional, institutional learning but must also take advantage of opportunities for less traditional education and life-long learning. Beginning with preschoolers and new parents, and continuing with the provision of materials and services that support learning for adults at all stages of life and learning, we must position our libraries to provide meaningful and high-quality services. To do this, the library needs 1 percent of the city's operating budget.

One percent for libraries is an investment in our future – it's an investment in our citizens. The "Information Age" will provide us all with challenges. Literacy and learning at all stages of life will be critical for both individual success and the success of our society. The Norfolk Public Library can make a difference. With 1 percent of the city's budget, our libraries can be a gateway to the information superhighway and to the avenues of learning, quiet study, contemplation, research, and enjoyment in the works and thoughts of others.

Can we afford to invest 1 percent in libraries? The real question is – can we afford not to?

Figure 3.13—(*Continued*)

TELEVISION COVERAGE

The newspaper is not the only mass medium that is available for promoting the library. Consider broadcast media as well. Television is probably the medium with the most penetration—depending on the channel. And, of course, the difficulty you will have in getting time on television will correlate directly with the viewership of that station. It may be easy to get time on the local community, campus, or school station but you will not reach many people that way. Getting time on public television or on a commercial channel is much more difficult but can be very effective.

There are several ways to gain coverage on television. One is to create a media event that is newsworthy or will sell well as a feature story on the six o'clock news. Don't hesitate to talk to the program and news editors of your local stations and find out what they would consider important enough to cover. Find out from them what they are looking for in terms of content and also days and times of the week that you may be more likely to get coverage. Be sure to get involved with the television station on the front end (before you create a media event or seek coverage for a special program) in order to introduce yourself, get buy-in from them, and heighten your chances for coverage in the first place.

Once you have a good relationship with the appropriate staff members of your local television stations consider the events coming up in your library that have good visual appeal and meet the criteria defined by the stations. Pitch the story to them. Let them know why it will be important for viewers and what will make it newsworthy and visually interesting. Realize that no matter how well you plan for coverage of an event, you will always be in competition with whatever else is happening at the time—planned or otherwise. If you have ascertained from your station the best times for coverage of events, you will have increased your chances. It's possible you will find out when their typical slow times are during the day or when there is a shift change at the station making news reporters unavailable except for emergencies.

As you pitch the story, be sure once again to let the station staff know how this issue or event fits into the larger issues of your organization. Let them know why this event or issue is important to everyone—not just the library and not just library supporters. If you are getting coverage of a special children's program, be sure to pitch the story as how your library plays an educational role in the lives of parents and their children. Talk about literacy and prevention. Talk about school success. Have supportive anecdotal evidence ready as well as standard statistics. Be excited about what you are asking the television station to cover, because enthusiasm sells.

Another way to get television coverage is to try to get personal airtime for an interview about library issues. Many cities, towns, schools, and campuses have a local television station that dedicates certain time slots during the week or month to local issues. If you have done a good job in establishing a relationship with the news media, you should not have too much trouble getting an interview. The only problem is that such local talk shows often have small audiences and they often air at noon or late at night. Although you are likely to get a good amount of time to talk about your library, you may not get the kind of audience that a story on the six o'clock news will get.

TIPS FOR SUCCESSFUL TELEVISION APPEARANCES

Whether you initiate television coverage or a library event or issue (sometimes controversial) brings the cameras to you, you can maximize the time you will get to make your point and send your message. The following tips will help you make the case for your library and enable you to leave the listener with a strong sense of what your message is:

- **Be Prepared!** If you initiate the coverage you will have plenty of time to prepare, and nothing will stand you in better stead than to feel completely in command of the information and message you wish to send. On the other hand, as your library becomes increasingly high profile in your community, it is possible that the camera crew will simply show up someday to investigate a news story (often controversial, if you didn't get any notice). Of course you can decline an interview if you didn't get notice and that may be the best recourse in some cases. However, if this is about a library policy issue, a pending referendum, or some other library matter that is not personal, you will probably do well to try to get your message across and mitigate any controversy to the best of your ability. "The director refused to comment," doesn't sound that great on the six o'clock news. Even if you had no warning, however, that doesn't mean you shouldn't be prepared. You know what issues might be controversial in your community and you know what your library's message is. *Don't panic.* Take a deep breath, remember the message, and use it to turn a potentially negative interview into a positive one. Your library's mission is to do good, to provide a unique and important service! You're one of the good guys, so let that guide your approach.

- **Be Repetitive.** Even if you get a full half-hour or an hour on a local news station that specializes in local issues, this is still a brief time, and your job is to leave the audience remembering one or two key points. In fact, it's unlikely they'll remember more than that. Decide ahead of time what you'd like everyone to remember, and bring the conversation back around to that issue or point several times throughout the interview (see **Bridge, Hook, and Flag** below).
- **Be Yourself.** The more relaxed and personal you come across, the more the audience will like you. The more your audience likes you, the more they will listen to what you say and believe in you and your cause. Speak conversationally—try to imagine that you are explaining things to your best friend.
- **Share Anecdotes.** Libraries have stories—lots of stories. Keep some of them in your mind and use them during an interview. Facts and figures are not memorable. They are fine for written reports, but they should be kept to a minimum during a television interview or during any speaking engagement. It is better to illustrate a point by showing how it matters, how it actually made a difference to a patron in your library.
- **Use Statistics** (if you must). Sometimes statistics are so compelling they can really make the case for your library—but they really should be kept to a minimum. If you are going to use them, try to put them into human context. For example, "67 percent of the people in this city use our library on a regular basis. That means that even if you don't use the library, it is likely that the neighbors on either side of you do," or, "87 percent of our student body used the library last year, triple the percent that attended a collegiate athletic event."
- **Bridge, Hook, and Flag.** These are three techniques for controlling the conversation or interview so that you are sure to convey to your audience the main point or points that you want remembered.

  Bridge. This technique will allow you to move from an area in the conversation that you don't want to discuss and get the conversation back to your message. If the reporter says, for example, "wouldn't it help the library if you began to charge user fees?" You can get the conversation back to your message by responding, "I think the real question is, how important is the library to the well-being of this community? If we can agree that lifelong learning is critical for individual success in the 21st century, then how can we afford *not* to fully fund libraries and certainly, funding the public library is an important governmental responsibility." This may even be a good time to follow up with a fact to emphasize the *value* of the library. You could finish by saying, "In fact, did you know that even though nearly 70 percent of our citizens use the library on a regular basis, only 1 percent of the city's operating budget is used for their funding?" The main thing is, you don't have to come up with this off the top of your head—you should be prepared with this bridging statement prior to your interview. Remember, *be prepared!*

Hook. This is a technique that gets the interviewer to follow up on your first point, allowing you to get a second point in. For example, you can say, "There are two very important considerations that must be taken into account before we support this proposed policy. The first is . . ." and then expand on that point. The interview will seem incomplete when aired if the reporter doesn't follow up with, "and the second point?" This is a good way to ensure that both your points get airtime.

Flag. This technique is the easiest, and most people use it unconsciously all the time. Flagging alerts your listeners to what you consider most important. It's a good way to emphasize the key point or points you want the audience to remember. Flagging is simply giving your audience a verbal clue about what is important: "The most important thing to remember is . . ." or "If you remember nothing else, please remember these two points . . . ."

- **Don't Repeat a Negative.** The reporter or interviewer might say something like, "Isn't the proposed increase for your library going to hurt the police department?" You don't want to repeat "hurt the police department," so your answer shouldn't be "our budget isn't big enough to hurt the police department." If you respond in this way, the audience has now heard "hurt the police department" twice and the reporter may repeat it to you again. Though this is a fairly common question asked of public library directors and it seems a difficult one on the surface, it's actually a soft ball. Instead of repeating the negative phrase, you can respond with, "In fact, most consider libraries part of the solution for public safety. We know that long-term education is the best means of crime prevention, but even in the short term, our library serves hundreds of teens after school every day, giving them something productive and fun to do and keeping them from being bored and on the streets."

- **Look Professional.** Remember, television is a visual medium and your presence will create an impression about you and your integrity. Even if you are a Birkenstock kind of person, for the interview dress professionally. A good rule of thumb would be to dress as if you were applying for a high-level job interview. Wear solid colors, minimize jewelry, and if the station crew isn't set to do make-up, be sure to put on a shine-reducing powder. Women should wear lipstick and blush that is darker than usual so the face doesn't fade under bright lights.

- **Stay Calm!** You're the expert here so relax and try to enjoy your opportunity to tell the library's story. Concentrate on speaking to the reporter or interviewer as a person and forget the camera and lights. Establish eye contact with him or her and keep an "open face" (no frowning, tight lips, or furrowed brows!). Soon you really will forget the camera and you will be getting that important message out there to everyone who's tuned in.

PUBLIC SERVICE ANNOUNCEMENTS

A public service announcement can be an effective way to get library visibility through television. If you are looking for free airtime, however, you might get stuck with a single showing at 3 a.m. on Sunday. Depending on how important this avenue is to you for getting your message out, you may want to find out what the best rates are for a public service announcement and when your message will reach the audience you want. You won't get prime time but that may not be the best time for your message. All television (and radio) stations keep information on user profiles for each segment of airtime. The audience you are trying to reach may be late Friday night viewers and you may be able to get a favorable rate for that time.

Of course, ensuring that a public service announcement on television is effective requires that you have a very good, eye-catching, announcement. Be sure to have such an announcement professionally produced. A plan to get the library's message out will backfire if your announcement is weak and amateurish. Contact a local public relations firm and work with them to develop an excellent video that effectively communicates your message if you are going to go this route.

Public service announcements for television are expensive—at least they will be if they are going to be effective. There is the cost of professional production and the cost of airtime (don't go to the trouble and expense of production if you are not willing to pay to get a decent time slot). Because of this expense, you may want to consider using television as a communications method only when you are engaged in a targeted campaign for funding or referendum. Plus, you may have a hard time convincing your administration that you need funding if you are producing library commercials for prime time!

While television public service announcements (PSA) may be out of reach, radio is often much more accessible. Professionally produced radio public service announcements are often very inexpensive. Work with a local radio station and disc jockey to design an ad or series of ads that promote your library and its importance and value to the listener. A good radio PSA will be catchy (including sound effects and music). It should be read by a professional radio announcer and should clearly convey what the library has to offer and why that is valuable.

In working with a radio station to develop a PSA be sure to brainstorm about the wide variety of services your library has and let them know what your desired outcome is. For ongoing advocacy, your desired outcome should be a community better educated about the important role your library plays in people's lives. Again, consider your audience. Who are you trying to educate? Who are you trying to influence? Discuss that with the people who are producing the PSA so they make the script appealing to that audience.

If you are developing a series of radio PSAs, be sure that they have a consistent "sound." They should all be read by the same person and have the same music and tag line. The goal for a radio PSA or series of PSAs should be to penetrate, to the best of your financial ability, the airwaves. If you do this, your spots will soon be recognizable and you will have gone a long way to "branding" your library and its value to those listening.

Once you have professionally produced PSAs you must make sure they get played. You might go with one overwhelmingly popular station (the one that produced the PSAs for you?) or you may select several to reach a more diverse audience. Radio stations are often more willing to give free airtime (and at a decent time of day) than television. But, even if you must pay for some time slots, you will find radio much cheaper than television. You may not be able to afford the most active listening times but you may be able to broker a deal to pay for a certain number of slots during the more affordable times in exchange for a few, high-listener slots as well.

In Figure 3.14 are the scripts from radio PSAs that were specially developed for my library. The producer put these together for $200 as a way of making a contribution to the library. Getting the airtime—both free and inexpensive—was an easy final step. The Friends of the Library can support this kind of promotional campaign and they can even tag on with the phone number for listeners who might want to join the Friends, doubling the value of their investment.

Sample Radio Ads

Generic

Where can you find . . .

Swashbuckling pirate . . . *(sound effects—sword play)*
The king of the jungle . . . *(sound effects—roar)*
Far away galaxies . . . *(sound effects—spaceship in flight)*

It's not a video game, it's the Norfolk Public Library. Let your imagination take you to the ends of the earth and beyond! It's easy. The Norfolk Public Library has it all . . . books, audio-recordings, videos. . . . If your imagination is hungry for adventure, drop the joystick and head to the library. You'll go farther.

For more information, contact the Norfolk Public Library at 555–READ. It's time to thrive.

Family Resources
(sound effects—happy baby)

Congratulations! You're now new parents. But, you have questions. Where do you go from here? The answers are waiting for you at the Norfolk Public Library.

New parents can find everything they need to know in the Norfolk Public Library's family resource centers. From prenatal to preschool, the family resource centers have books and videos to give parents the information and guidance they need to raise healthy, happy kids. Find the answers you need. All it takes is your free library card and a trip to the Norfolk Public Library.

For more information, contact the Norfolk Public Library at 555–READ. It's time to thrive!

Technology

Welcome to the age of Web sites, megabytes, and modems. Today's technology is growing exponentially and computer knowledge is a must. Let the Norfolk Public Library be your on-ramp to computers and the information superhighway.

Just because you don't own a computer doesn't mean you can't take advantage of all they have to offer. At the Norfolk Public Library you'll find computers with Internet access, CD-ROMs and educational software, even computer classes and training. You'll soon find that hard drives aren't hard at all.

For more information, contact the Norfolk Public Library at 555–READ. It's time to thrive.

Employment

Thinking of changing careers? Can't find the information you need to decide which job is right for you? The answers you seek are waiting for you at the Norfolk Public Library.

In today's thriving market, finding a job is easy. But finding the job that's right for you takes a little effort. The skills you need to get ahead, information about specific companies, resume and interview skills help. If you have questions about employment, the answers you seek are waiting for you at the Norfolk Public Library.

For more information, contact the Norfolk Public Library at 555–READ. It's time to thrive!

Figure 3.14—Sample radio ads, Rod Duren Productions.

These public service announcements show how the library supports all types of learning for all types of people. A consistent music track and a consistent "tag line" makes them immediately identifiable to the listener and helps to "brand" the library.

GENERAL PROMOTIONAL PIECES

Flyers, bookmarks, notepads, posters—all these are traditional ways in which the library has communicated its services to its constituents. They're cheap and effective ways to get your message out. Just like the library newsletter, these communication tools can be used to both inform your public about what you have to offer and impart the importance of your library in general.

Be sure to maximize the value of every single public relations effort, every single promotional device by promoting the library's value as well as its services. Many libraries have been successful in designing their own clever, eye-catching materials to promote their library. In addition to the one-time promotion of events or services, you can make a more long-lasting impression about your library by publishing give-away materials that the recipient can use. Figures 3.15–3.25 are samples of a notepad and of a Post-it notepad that can be given away (along with other promotional materials) to the audience at speaking engagements; to city, campus, or corporate leaders; and to others who have or may have an interest in your library.

Figure 3.15—Post-it note, Information Today, Inc.

These Post-it notes (enlarged here for emphasis) allow for wide and easy distribution and boldly and simply proclaim that "Libraries are Essential."

"Whatever the cost of our libraries, the price is cheap compared to that of an ignorant nation."

-Walter Cronkite

Figure 3.16—Notepad, Norfolk (Va.) Public Library.

Easily produced and inexpensive, a notepad with a high-profile endorsement of libraries gets the word out every time it is used.

The libraries of America are and must ever remain the home of free, inquiring minds.

Dwight D. Eisenhower

Books, videos, cassettes, the Internet, and other formats contain a vast universe of information and ideas. The Dauphin County Library System is committed to providing access to that universe for all people, regardless of age, race, religion, gender, physical ability or economic status.

Parents, you are the best and final judge of what is appropriate for your own children. Please guide them in using and borrowing library resources.

Dauphin County Library System

Figure 3.17—Bookmark, Dauphin County (Pa.) Library System.

Effective use of a powerful quote on a bookmark gives library services cache and ensures that the message can be widely disseminated.

100 Ways to Light Your Way to the Future at the Queens Borough Public Library

LIGHTING THE WAY
1896 • 1996

FIND

the tallest mountain
a volunteer opportunity
the richest American
the best company to work for
a college for your child
a chocaholics cookbook
exhibits and art works
the fastest way to San Jose
a bus route to Brooklyn
the World Wide Web
the value of your baseball card collection
scholarships
grants
awards
an inn in Innsbruck
a gopher in Queens
a guru in Brooklyn

MAHOOD

ng mga katutubong sayan mula Sa Pilipinas

DEVELOP

your resume
a French accent
photographs and an artist's eye
the right (or left) side of your brain
your sense of humor
a repertoire of stories,

songs and monologues
patience
understanding
compassion and wisdom
a new attitude
a body to match it

ESCUCHE

los audio-libros en espanol

LEARN

How to say no
another language
parenting
sign language
the history of Queens
origami
English as a Second Language
counting and accounting
who, what, when, where and how
how to use InfoLinQ
how to find it on the computer
to read and write
low fat cookery
flower arranging
handicapping horses and golf
who was who and when she was what she was
about first ladies, second basemen, and third wheels

Figure 3.18—Bookmark, Queens Borough (N.Y.) Public Library.

More than just a list of services, this bookmark informs patrons that library services "Light the Way to the Future."

Figure 3.19—Bookmark, Fairfax County (Va.) Public Library.

This bookmark points out that materials *and* staff combine to make services meaningful on an individual by individual basis.

CLASP: Connecting Libraries and Schools Project

Reading is the fundamental building block of learning in our society. A child who cannot read is at a serious disadvantage. Despite the efforts and concerns of educators nationwide, acquiring basic literacy skills remains the single most critical problem among our schoolchildren.

Our schools cannot bear the full burden for developing reading skills in young people. Meeting this challenge requires the cooperation of parents, caregivers, teachers, community groups . . . *and libraries.*

Bill Higgins

1

Figure 3.20—CLASP brochure, New York (N.Y.), Queens Borough (N.Y.), and Brooklyn (N.Y.) Public Libraries.

This brochure is clear about why reading matters and states clearly that reading success "requires libraries."

Figure 3.21—Brochure, Harford (Md.) Public Library.

Connecting Einstein to libraries constitutes an effective endorsement and links libraries with intellectual achievement.

Figure 3.22—Brochure, Youngstown and Mahoning County (Ohio) Library.

The title of this brochure says it all!

Read Your Way To The Top

King County Library System
1999 Summer Reading Program
June 26 - August 7

Young Adults ages 12-18:

Read a book, magazine or newspaper. Or listen to a book on cassette, watch a video, or listen to music. You choose.

Write a short review of what you read, heard or saw. You'll find free entry forms at all KCLS libraries. Complete one review/entry for each item you choose.

Turn in your entries each week in the entry box or at any King County Library System branch. Each library will hold a prize drawing every week. Final entries due August 7.

A grand prize drawing will happen in mid-August.

www.kcls.org

Figure 3.23—Bookmark, King County (Wash.) Library System.

The implication is clear: reading (and libraries) will take you to the top.

Figure 3.24—Brochure, The Free Library of Philadelphia, Pa.

This brochure effectively shows the *value* of a library card.

The Fairfax County Public Library

Library

Here is where people,
One frequently finds,
Lower their voices
And raise their minds.

Richard Armour
-Light Armour.
McGraw-Hill, 1954.

The Center for the Book exists to stimulate public interest in and to celebrate the importance of books and reading in Fairfax County and Fairfax City.

The Center for the Book is affiliated with the Virginia Center for the Book, and is supported by grants, donations, corporations, and gifts from individuals. Its activities are supplemented by in-kind contributions and volunteers.

The Center's activities include forming partnerships with private and public entities to advance books and reading through literary events, author appearances, public and corporate workshops, expositions, discussion series, seminars, and other programs and events related to books and reading.

"The current definitive answer to almost any question can be found within the four walls of most libraries."

Arthur Ashe

Figure 3.25—Brochure, Fairfax County (Va.) Public Library

This brochure focuses on purpose as well as services and uses quotes to underline the importance of libraries.

In addition, the American Library Association publishes clip art each year in concert with national library events and programs. These materials are made freely available to the library community, they are professional, and are almost always copyright free. They usually include the message that libraries matter, that libraries change lives. Use these materials and make them even more meaningful by tying in your library's own message.

Figures 3.26–3.35 are samples of clip art that ALA makes available for general library promotion as well as the promotion of special library promotional events. ALA's promotional materials are often based on presidential initiatives and focus on the important role that libraries play in our society.

Figures 3.26—Clip art, American Library Association.

Libraries are the connection many kids have to the Internet and that connection can open doors to the world.

Figures 3.27—Clip art, American Library Association.

What could be more important to a child's development than a passport to lifelong learning?

Figures 3.28—Clip art, American Library Association.

Libraries make a difference, libraries matter, because libraries change lives.

Figures 3.29—Clip art, American Library Association.

Know your audience! These materials are eye-catching and relevant to young adults.

American Library Association ▪ Public Information Office ▪ 50 E. Huron St. ▪ Chicago, IL 60611 ▪ 312-280-5043

Figures 3.30—Clip art, American Library Association.

The powerful message that libraries change lives works for any type of library.

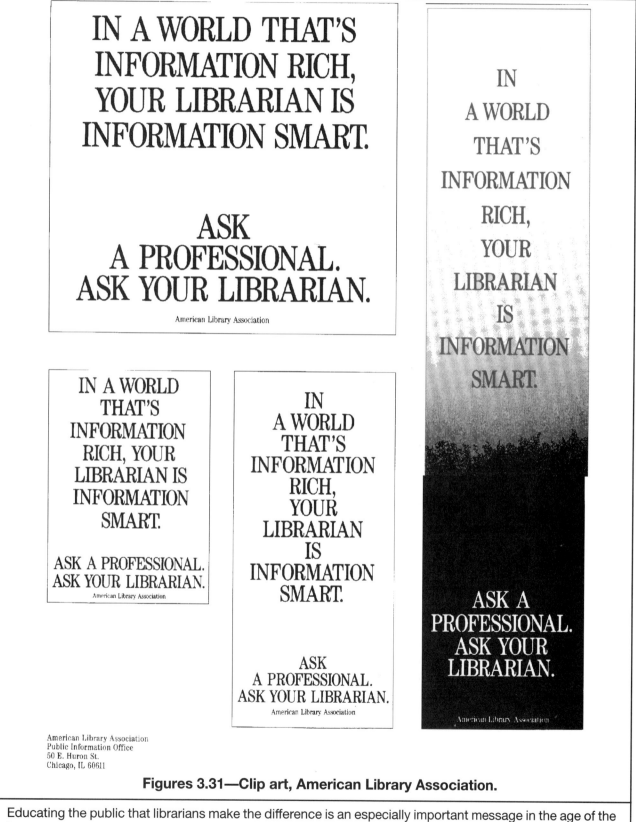

American Library Association
Public Information Office
50 E. Huron St.
Chicago, IL 60611

Figures 3.31—Clip art, American Library Association.

Educating the public that librarians make the difference is an especially important message in the age of the Internet.

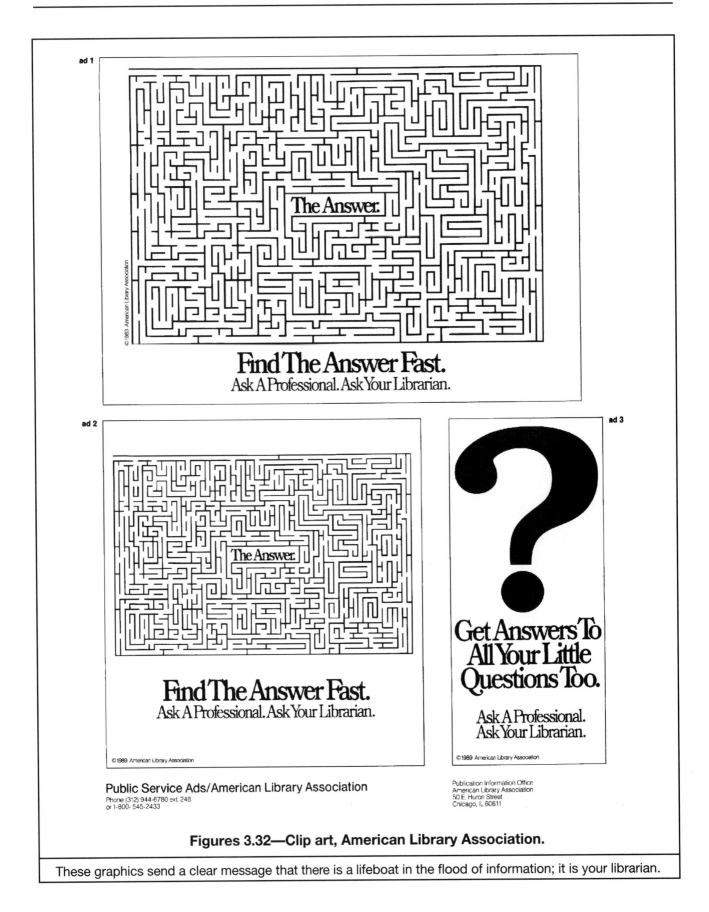

Figures 3.32—Clip art, American Library Association.

These graphics send a clear message that there is a lifeboat in the flood of information; it is your librarian.

It's small enough to fit in your wallet, powerful enough to change your life...
It's a library card.

Learn how to help your children do better in school, be a better parent, do better on a job interview, save money on home repairs, find a job, start your own business.

Your librarian will be glad to help.
Get your library card today.

Warning:
A library card can change your life.

Get your library card today.

American
Library
Association

LIBRARY CARD

Tan pequeña que cabe en su billetera...¡Tan potente que puede cambiarle la vida!
Es una tarjeta de biblioteca.

Aprenda cómo... ayudar a sus hijos a mejorar en la escuela, ser un mejor padre, presentarse mejor en una entrevista, ahorrar dinero en reparaciones del hogar, encontrar trabajo, iniciar su propio negocio.

A su bibliotecario le agradará poder ayudarle.
Obtenga su tarjeta de biblioteca hoy mismo.

Advertencia:
Una tarjeta de biblioteca puede cambiarle la vida.

Asociación
Americana
de Bibliotecas

TARJETA DE BIBLIOTECA

It's small enough to fit in your wallet... powerful enough to change your life!

Get your library card today.

American
Library
Association

LIBRARY CARD

Tan pequeña que cabe en su billetera... ¡Tan potente que puede cambiarle la vida!

Obtenga su tarjeta de biblioteca hoy mismo.

Asociación
Americana
de Bibliotecas

TARJETA DE BIBLIOTECA

American Library Association ▪ Public Information Office ▪ 50 E. Huron St. ▪ Chicago, IL 60611 ▪ 312-280-5043

Figures 3.33—Clip art, American Library Association.

It's important that the library's message is directed to the *entire* audience and reflects the community's diversity.

Public Service Ads
American Library Association

For special size/film/
 color specs, contact:
Public Information Office
American Library Association
50 E. Huron St.
Chicago, IL 60611

(312) 944-6780 ext. 248/
1-800-545-2433

The Best Gift
You'll Ever Give Your Child.

A gift that won't break, won't wear out,
won't be outgrown.
Educational and fun for all ages.
Free of charge
at a location near you.

A Library Card*

HOMETOWN LIBRARY CARD

*No batteries required.

AMERICAN LIBRARY ASSOCIATION

Figures 3.34—Clip art, American Library Association.

A library card offers the gift of learning for all occasions and it's free! What a powerful concept!

Support your library.

American Library Association

Public Service Ads
American Library Association

Contact: Public Information Office (312) 280-5043
American Library Association 50 E. Huron St. Chicago, IL 60611

Figures 3.35—Clip art, American Library Association.

This makes a good strong case for support even in tough economic times.

ANNUAL REPORTS

Most libraries are required to publish an annual report. The degree to which libraries use this opportunity to provide a glossy, professional promotional piece versus using this vehicle as a simple business tool to report on the year's activities varies dramatically. I am not sure if the degree to which a library spends money and time to "look good" really pays off unless the report is eye-catching, brief on text, heavy on photos, and quick to make the point that what libraries do matters and that libraries should be fully funded. Figures 3.36–3.43 are examples of annual reports that communicate the message effectively.

Some libraries use the annual report to provide information on performance as well as to promote the library all year long. Notepads and calendars are two such methods that can be effective. Along with keeping the library's name in front of people longer (as in a calendar or notepad), you can use the opportunity with such devices to sell the library's importance as well.

As with your newsletter, be sure that you get all the exposure for your library as possible from the annual report. Send it to those who might not think of the library throughout the year but who are influential and you want to cultivate. Again, be sure that you have developed a VIP mailing list and send your annual report to everyone on that list.

Statistics

Annual Circulation

Grove City Library	442,963
Westland Area Library	398,015
Bookmobile/Outreach	99,910
System Total	940,888

Reference Questions

62,505

Program Attendance

17,545

Volunteer Hours

In 1993, a total of **70** volunteers worked **3,692 hours**. In 1994, a total of **185** volunteers worked **4,924 hours**, a 25% increase over 1993.

This includes regular volunteers, library shoppe workers, summer reading program teens, community service teens, Girl Scouts, Friends of the Library and Trustees.

An additional **40** volunteers assisted with the Yes & KNOW Committee for the levy campaign in 1994.

Financial Report

REVENUES	1994 Actual
State Income Taxes	$2,671,196
General Property Taxes	0
Patron Fines and Fees	85,953
Interest	8,466
Gifts	11,397
Other Income	16,299
	$2,793,311

EXPENDITURES	
Salaries and Benefits	$1,708,839
Supplies	54,963
Purchased Services	661,932
Library Materials	341,981
Capital Outlay	39,012
Other	3,399
	$2,810,126

*This is an **unaudited** statement.*

From the Director

In our first full year of participation in the Discovery Place consortium, Southwest Public Libraries loaned ten books, videos, recordings and other items for every resident of the South-Western City School District. That million items loaned included more than 50,000 not available from our own collections but obtained through the Discovery Place reserve system. Meanwhile, our librarians answered more than 60,000 questions and assisted thousands of area residents onto the Information Superhighway with the advent of the Greater Columbus FreeNet. Our summer reading program, the biggest ever, involved some 3,500 children and preteens. Overall, it was another year of excellent library service to our community.

Yet, it is difficult to present in a totally positive light, a year when the library was suffering the cumulative effects of eroding state funding; a year when growth in that funding was again so minimal that utilities, insurance and similar operating costs consumed every dollar of increase, leaving little to purchase new library materials, and none to fill vacant staff positions, implement new technologies, or even replace deteriorating equipment; a year when voters turned down a modest request for local tax dollars while continuing to increase demands on the library system for service. Sadly, 1994 ended with plans to trim an already lean budget and curtail a few more basic services in order to begin a new cycle of attempting to do more with less as we respond to our customers' needs.

Frances Black
Library Director

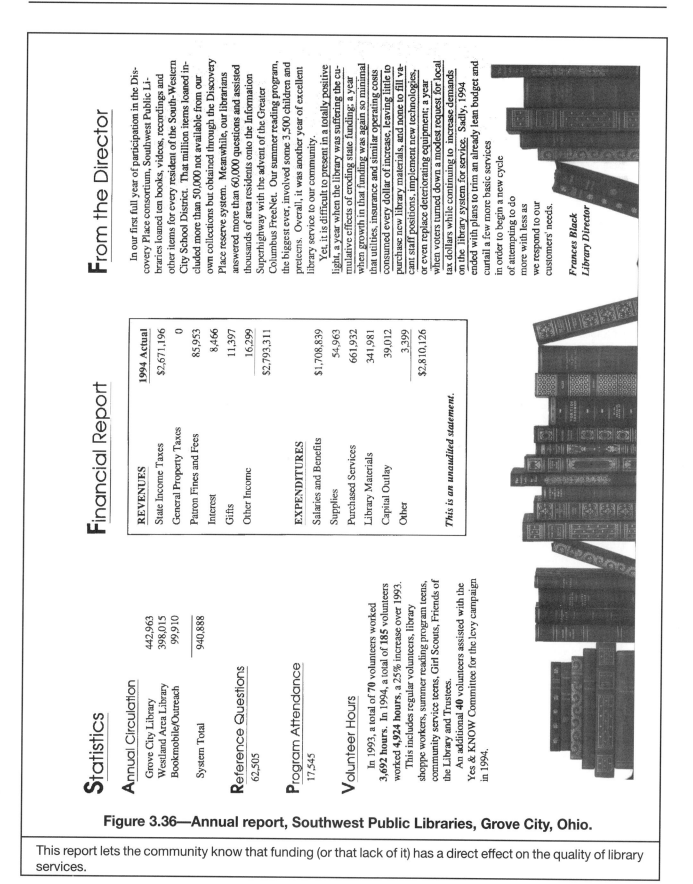

Figure 3.36—Annual report, Southwest Public Libraries, Grove City, Ohio.

This report lets the community know that funding (or that lack of it) has a direct effect on the quality of library services.

Libraries change lives. And, nourish creativity, open minds, and fire imaginations. Libraries provide information to those with inquiring minds, to those seeking solutions to today's problems, and to those planning for tomorrow's careers. Libraries help preserve the past and offer help on how to use the newest information technology.

The King County Library System, through its 39 community branches and on-line services, strives to keep pace with the information needs of nearly one million customers. In 1995, the pace of change was rapid: an interlibrary delivery network replaced the books-by-mail system, four libraries opened, installation of a wide area network offered more lines of information, and new programs were launched.

In early 1995, Slick! (Speedy Library Info Checkout) replaced the long-standing, popular books-by-mail service. In response to a skyrocket increase in postage costs, the library system implemented an interlibrary delivery system for reserved titles. The goal: to maintain free, open, and equal access while delivering materials quickly, efficiently, and equitably.

Customers flocked into libraries to pick up over one million holds during the year. Circulation reached an all-time high, with 12.7 million items checked out (a 3% increase over the previous year). This tally placed King County Library System as the second busiest circulating library in the United States.

I sure miss having books mailed to me, but if it's a choice between that and funding for on-line service, I'll pick up my books.
John Spinosa
Bellevue Regional Library

The switch to Slick! saved nearly $500,000 and showed that the strength of the system is in its collection of over 3 million items and in its ability to deliver information. New materials added in 1995 included CD-ROMS for check out and for use in libraries, and on-line databases including American Heritage Dictionary, National Newspaper Index, Community Resource File, ProQuest, PhoneDisc USA, and other titles.

Connecting to the library (InfoNet) from homes and offices grew in use. In 1995, there were 728,000 modem and dial-up connections (2,000 a day or more than one every minute), a 54% increase over 1994.

To ensure that the on-line system will remain relevant, a wide area network was installed which replaced communication equipment throughout all libraries. This change enabled faster response time and broader bandwidth to accommodate new information transmissions. With this in place, magazine articles and indexes on-line are scheduled in 1996, as well as additional Internet connections and other services.

This system is extraordinary. It is, to me, almost miraculous that I can think of almost any book, and have it in my hands within a week or two.
Rick McClurg
Shoreline Library

Library staff members are the link between the information seeker and the information sought. And, to enhance their skills, all reference staff participated in SMART training (Skills for More Adept Reference Transactions) - training useful in answering 1.2 million reference questions, a 7% increase over 1994.

Volunteers and staff developed workshops, trainings and 'techno fairs' to help the uninitiated learn (and master) how to surf the Internet, search The Catalog, and track down data.

The Interlibrary Loan staff have been very helpful. Their work makes King County citizens' access to information limitless.
Marty Gale
Mercer Island Library

Libraries and Literacy

The technology in libraries is important to many in the community. Yet, there are others for whom learning to read is a major accomplishment. The library system provides staff and collections and works with community agencies to accomplish this goal. In 1995, two key alliances were developed to further these efforts. KCLS provided office space for the King County Literacy Coalition and collaborated on programs. And, KCLS teamed up with Americorps and supported a literacy outreach person who promoted library services and programs to adult

Figure 3.37—Annual report, King County (Wash.) Library System.

This library has taken the opportunity to show how libraries are making a difference for life-long learning.

Step back in time more than four decades and catch the vision of Betty Snowden Patterson, principal of the Nathan C. Schaeffer School and later the Camp Hill Civic Club's Literature Committee. Together, these fine folks dreamed of creating a community library, a place to bring together people and resources. The result? Establishment of the Camp Hill Public Library on September 17, 1957. When its doors opened at the American Legion Building on South 22nd Street in Camp Hill, 4,000 books lined its shelves.

In July 1960, the library moved into new quarters under the stage of the Camp Hill High School Auditorium — but not for long. Just five years later, the Camp Hill Public Library's Board of Trustees entered into an agreement with William M. and Clara Hollinger to purchase property for the purpose of building a new library. Within one week, the name was changed to the West Shore Public Library. And on October 17, 1967, the new $317,000 library opened at 30 North 31st Street, Camp Hill. Its East Pennsboro Branch was established on October 7, 1985.

In 1991, Foresight, Inc. conducted a Needs Assessment which recommended the West Shore Public Library at least double the size of its current facility. The resulting capital campaign proposes a goal of $6.4 million for the new facility.

The West Shore Public Library is one of seven libraries within the Cumberland County Library System, each with its own governing Board of Trustees. The West Shore Public Library's Board of Trustees consists of 13 elected members and 6 members appointed from the municipalities served by the library.

Its state mandated service area is: Camp Hill Borough, East Pennsboro Township, Hampden Township, Lemoyne Borough, Lower Allen Township, and Wormleysburg Borough.

Cleve J. Fredricksen, a former chairman of AMP, Inc., was actively involved in the Harrisburg community for many years. One of the founders of the West Shore Public Library in 1957, Mr. Fredricksen contributed the seed money for the current library building in the mid 1960s.

Known for his generosity and commitment to the Harrisburg area, he established the Fredricksen Foundation in 1987, with the mission of supporting health care, human services and educational institutions in the Greater Harrisburg area.

We are very grateful for a generous gift of $1,000,000 from the Fredricksen Foundation by his widow, Mary Jane Fredricksen, made with the stipulation that the library be named for her late husband. A matching grant of $1,000,000 from the Whitaker Foundation provides generous support for this project, as well as another AMP connection. We are pleased that our new facility will memorialize Mr. Fredricksen's name and honor his years of service to the community in a fitting way.

Figure 3.38—Annual report, West Shore Public Library, Camp Hill, Pa.

This annual report shows how the library has continued to grow and continued to meet community needs over time—a successful investment.

Ames Public Library
ANNUAL REPORT
1998·1999

x TRADITION
x EXPLORATION
x INNOVATION

LIBRARY³

AMES PUBLIC LIBRARY
515 DOUGLAS AVE. AMES, IA 50010-6215
www.ames.lib.ia.us

*"Not everything
that can be counted
counts, and
not everything
that counts
can be counted."*
· *Albert Einstein* ·

HIGHLIGHTS OF THE YEAR

❑ Dedication of "A World to Teach" sculpture by Jane Dedecker: A gift of Michael and Barbara Gartner in memory of their son, Christopher. *May 1999*

❑ Installation of two 3M SelfCheck™ stations: Gifts of the Ames Public Library Foundation and 3M Company. *August 1999*

❑ Installation of a new 3M security system. *October 1998*

❑ Renovation of Circulation Services adds another check-out station and display space for nonprint materials. With check-out consolidated at one service point, Media Services takes on a new role. Media staff will help customers discover what the Library offers for listening, viewing and computing activities.

❑ Enrich Iowa funding passes the Iowa legislature giving state aid to libraries – Ames Public Library's share is over $11,000.

POPULATION SERVED   56,994

Ames	48,691
Gilbert (by contract)	796
Rural Story County (by contract)	7,507

Figure 3.39—Annual report, Ames (Iowa) Public Library.

This simple and readable annual report begins with a quote by Einstein to remind the community that a library's importance transcends quantifiable measures.

Our new library features:

Community
meeting rooms

First floor art gallery

Queuing line at checkout

Parking lot entrance

Alley book drop

The Mouse House

Quiet study rooms

Solar system mural

Quiet reading room

Children's program room

Parenting collection

Child-size display cases

Multimedia computers

Child-size entrance
to the Junior Room

All adult materials
on one floor

Teen Central area

Western collection

Computer rooms

Biography collection

Color copier

Short story collection

New Conference Room

and offers more:

Study seating

Lounge seating

Computer catalogs

Copy machines

Internet workstations

Computerized resources

"Our community's commitment to life long learning started a century ago with the Ladies Library Association. This facility begins the second century."

Downers Grove Public Library
1998 - 1999 Annual Report

Figure 3.40—Annual report, Downers Grove (Ill.) Public Library.

An opening quote in this report connects the importance of life-long learning to a proud library history.

Jesse Hoyt's Legacy

Jesse Hoyt

Jesse Hoyt was a prominent New York businessman with extensive property interests in East Saginaw. At his death in 1882, he left $100,000 for the establishment of a public library.

"I desire...a suitable and substantial building, to be used as a library and reading room for the use of young people of good character and habits."

Hoyt felt that some portion of the expenses of the library should be borne by the City. When it was suggested that $100,000 was inadequate to build and operate a library, he replied, "No, that should be enough. If the people want more than that will accomplish, then they ought to provide it."

The legacy continues...

Bruce L. Dalrymple
President, Hoyt Trust

If Jesse Hoyt were to peruse this booklet, he would be gratified to know that his legacy lives on and that it has been enhanced by the contributions of tens of thousands of others who did, indeed, want more than his legacy alone would have been able to accomplish. In less than five years, the library which he envisioned will have operated through a span encompassing three centuries. We can now celebrate the conclusion of the complete renovation of the Hoyt Public Library which both preserves its historical charm and prepares it for the operations of a first class library in the 21st century.

These substantial and necessary improvements were greatly assisted by the contributions of the Harvey Randall Wickes Foundation, The Herbert H. and Grace A. Dow Foundation, the Saginaw Community Foundation, the Rollin M. Gerstacker Foundation in Memory of Mary Dow, the Arnold and Gertrude Boutell Memorial Fund administered by Citizens Bank, the Morley Foundation and The Alden and Vada Dow Family Foundations. Additionally, hundreds of area residents provided substantial support to this renovation through individual contributions. Of course, the willingness of the voters of our district to pass a millage at a level appropriate to the maintenance of fine library facilities was crucial to the success of the project as well. Finally, the Library Board greatly appreciates the patience and cheerfulness exhibited by staff and patrons in the face of numerous inconveniences and disruptions necessarily occasioned by such a major undertaking.

As a result of all these contributions, this old building is now a fully functioning modern library as well. It stands as an enduring monument to the gift of Jesse Hoyt to this community and to the commitment of the community to expanding excellence in library service and facilities.

Figure 3.41—Annual report, Renovation Project, Public Libraries of Saginaw, Mich.

Sharing a sense of history can create a greater sense of pride and support for a library's future.

REACHING OUT TO... CHILDREN

In the words of Denver Mayor Wellington Webb,

"Kids and families are the heart of Denver. They keep us strong. They renew us. As the children grow, so grows Denver."

In 1999, children found hundreds of ways to stretch, grow and have plenty of fun, too, at the Denver Public Library.

The 1999 Children's Summer of Reading, for example, featured summer-long events co-sponsored by the Denver Public Library and its partner, the Denver Art Museum. The program, titled Art Tells a Story, inspired half of Denver's elementary school children to read for fun and prizes. Other outreach ventures included the award-winning After School is Cool program, which brought fun, educational activity and homework help to nine branch libraries and Book Babies, which brought sounds and song to the under-2-year-old set.

In 1999, Denver Public School teachers borrowed more than 800 multi-book teacher sets from Central and branch libraries to use in their classrooms. The Library also delivered Read at Home storybooks to daycare centers. From there, kids and their parents borrowed the books informally to read at home for extended periods without overdue fines.

Figure 3.42—Annual report, Denver (Colo.) Public Library.

Connecting the library to the city leadership's priorities gives the library instant clout.

The new bookmobile delivers the joy and power of books and reading to children, teens, seniors, and others who may not have easy access to one of the fourteen community libraries.

A   U N I V E R S E   W I T H I N   R E A C H

The library is a universe where the life of the mind dances, a space where learning is boundless, a journey toward the stars—transforming lives, leading to knowledge.

C O N N E C T I N G   T O   N E W   W O R L D S

The journey to knowledge increasingly depends on computerized connections that bring new worlds of information into reach. Combined with books and other media, electronic formats of information are expanding the library's ability to serve the educational and informational needs of our populace.

Libraries across the country are taking a leadership role in ensuring equity of access to electronic information. As an investment in the educational and economic future of Minneapolis, MPL devoted a portion of 1995 operating funds to strengthening the library's information technology capacity. In addition, a share of federal dollars earmarked for automation improvements was allocated to MPL through the Metropolitan Library Service Agency (MELSA), the federated system of public libraries in the seven-county area.

Through a strategic planning process and the work of Technology Initiatives Staff Teams, plans were underway by year's end to construct a new technology infrastructure, including a new telecommunications system, an internal network, upgraded equipment, public Internet access, and a new integrated library automation system. The realization of these plans will position the library as a pivotal institution for bringing cyberspace down to earth and within reach for everyone in the community.

Figure 3.43—Annual report, Minneapolis (Minn.) Public Library.

Libraries are "leaders" and are a "must" for the educational and economic future of the community.

ENDORSEMENTS

Promotional pieces often include quotes from nationally or internationally known persons who exhort the importance of libraries or the values that libraries espouse. Using quotes is a powerful way to convey the importance of libraries articulately and to suggest more subtly that persons of importance are library supporters and endorse the importance of libraries. Quotes often get read even if nothing else in your promotional material does. They are usually succinct, to the point, and repeatable.

We go to a lot of trouble to write articles, develop program brochures, publish annual reports. By adding a quote or two that addresses the message you are trying to convey and by highlighting and attributing that quote, you may find that you can make an impression about the value of libraries even if not all your materials get read by everyone.

Figure 3.44 offers quotes on libraries compiled by the American Library Assocation. The quotes are excellent for helping to make the case for your library in whatever venue you are using—written or spoken.

"My love for learning was fostered and enhanced by all the resources I made use of in the libraries where I studied . . . Today, the library is not only a special place for me but for my family as well. The library has made a difference in my life. I hope others will discover the library and let it change their lives."

• President Bill Clinton

"When I was young, we couldn't afford much. But, my library card was my key to the world. Have fun—READ"

• John Goodman, actor

"The library is a place that one can go and get the answers to virtually any questions they may have. It is a place that everyone should utilize frequently during their lives. The people need to support their public libraries in any way possible."

• Vincent E. "Bo" Jackson, athlete

"I was one of those kids for whom my neighborhood public library was a special haven. I cannot think of a time in my life—even in the dark days of law school—when a library didn't exert a potent attraction for me, offering a sense of the specialness of each individual's curiosity and his or her quest to satisfy it."

• Scott F. Turow, author

"Libraries are not basic—they're essential. If politicians want to save money, they should fund libraries."

• Patricia Glass Schuman, President, ALA 1991–1992

" . . . it's hypocritical, stupid and ridiculous to talk about the importance of quality education when they're closing libraries."

• U.S. Rep. Major Owens, D-NY

"Defend your local library as if your freedom depended on it."

• John Jakes, author

"It is virtually impossible to conceive of a literate and civilized society without libraries."

• U.S. Senator Alan Simpson

"Our libraries serve as the school rooms for a lifetime of learning—and the launching pads for our future."

• President George H. W. Bush

"Kids who read succeed. Those who don't won't. Neither will our country."

• Richard M. Dougherty, President, ALA, 1990–1991

"As one of six children, I distinguished myself academically at an early age by spending many hours in the library. Libraries work as partners for education with all levels of learning institutions."

• Maynard Jackson, former mayor of Atlanta

"Public libraries have been a mainstay of my life. They represent an individual's right to acquire knowledge; they are the sinews that bind civilized societies the world over. Without libraries, I would be a pauper, intellectually and spiritually. I cherish libraries."

• James A. Michener, author

"As a child, my number one best friend was the librarian in my grade school. I actually believed all those books belonged to her. . . . When she warned that some of these books were too old for me, I told her they were for my mother. I have never regretted my dishonesty."

• Erma Bombeck, columnist and author

"Libraries are absolutely at the center of my life. Since I couldn't afford to go to college, I attended the library three or four days a week from the age of eighteen on, and graduated from the library when I was twenty-eight. When I speak to students, I tell them 'It's no use going to school if the library is not your final goal.' That's how important it is for everyone and has been for me."

• Ray Bradbury, author

"The free access to information is not a privilege, but a necessity for any free society . . . One of my favorite things to do as a young man was wander through the stacks of my hometown library. I'd just browse until I found something interesting. Libraries have definitely changed my life."

• Edward Asner, actor

"I read myself out of poverty long before I worked myself out. Kids who read succeed. It was a librarian who showed me the way. Librarians change more lives than they know."

• Walter Anderson, Editor-in-Chief, Parade Magazine

"From doing debate research in my high school library in Waco, Texas, to visiting the Library of Congress in Washington with my children, libraries have always held a special place in my heart. They represent to me a place to go not only for knowledge, but for serenity. In this information age we live in, it is vital that we support our public libraries and take advantage of the services that they offer."

• Ann Richards, former Governor of Texas

"We all know that libraries are the fountain of knowledge, bubbling up history, science, the arts and a wealth of information for all. During my formative years, I always thought of the library when I wanted to know more about anything. Librarians have always been among the most thoughtful and helpful people. They are teachers without a classroom. No libraries, no progress."

• Willard Scott, TV personality

Figure 3.44—Quotes, compiled by the American Library Association.

You can make the quotes you use even more meaningful locally if leaders in your own community will comment on the value of libraries to them; you can then quote them in your publications and addresses. Politicians, administrators, campus and community leaders are often giving "lip service" to their support of libraries. Write down their remarks and use them as an opening in your next newsletter article—or in the promotional calendar your library produces. Highlight the mayor's remarks about his support of libraries in your next budget report or on the cover of your annual report. Using quotes is like getting a celebrity endorsement for your library and its services.

My favorite library quote comes from Toni Morrison, speaking at the New York Public Library in September, 1997:

Access to knowledge is the superb, the supreme act of truly great civilizations. Of all of the institutions that purport to do this, free libraries stand virtually alone in accomplishing this mission. No committee decides who may enter, no crisis of body or spirit must accompany the entrant. No tuition is charged, no oath sworn, no visa demanded. Of the monuments humans build for themselves, very few say "touch me, use me, my hush is not indifference, my space is not barrier. If I inspire awe, it is because I am in awe of you and the possibilities that dwell in you."

PRESENTATIONS

Nothing will get the message out better than a good, effective, personal presentation. You and everyone on staff who is good at public speaking should be charged with getting out into the community or campus to make the case in person. Libraries are important, and you and your staff, trustees, and Friends need to be sure that you get that message out individually. The opportunities for doing so are enormous if you are willing to pick up the phone and start calling.

Civic groups, service agencies, academic and city groups all need to know how libraries are important to them. They need to know how the library affects their lives, whether they use it or not. Nothing will convey this message better than a personal appearance by someone who understands the message and believes in it. Call the leaders of the various groups that meet routinely and ask them for time on their agenda at an upcoming meeting. You will be surprised at how accommodating most will be. The fact that libraries have universal appeal will help you get your foot in the door and then you will have the opportunity to make your services meaningful to your audience.

Getting the library's message out to those in your community who can influence library funding is an important and, hopefully, ongoing priority. In many libraries, however, staff trained and responsible for making effective presentations is limited or nonexistent. Although librarians are becoming increasingly aware of the critical importance of being outspoken library advocates, public speaking does not come naturally to everyone; our message is compelling, but our talent in delivering that message varies greatly.

Not only is the quality of the presentation and its delivery important, it is also critical that everyone speaking out on behalf of your library deliver a consistent message—that everyone knows and speaks "the party line."

See Chapter 4 for a detailed discussion of effective visual presentations.

INSTITUTIONALIZE PUBLIC RELATIONS

Sadly, when libraries restructure or downsize to accommodate budget cuts or to free up money for programs and services, they often look first to eliminating their office for public relations. By the same token, many libraries have never had a public relations person on board and they consider the idea a luxury or superfluous. In fact the very support you need to keep your budget healthy and keep libraries a priority in the minds of those who fund you will largely depend on the effectiveness of your public relations efforts.

Obviously any library engaged in promoting its services is engaged in public relations. For many of these libraries, this role is included in the job description of librarians already on board, such as those in youth services, adult services, or administration. The fact that it's included in someone's duties is, at least, an indication that it is considered to have some importance. It is the rare library, however, that can do an effective job of promotion (especially politically powerful promotion) without someone specially designated for that role. For larger libraries, a department of public relations or communications is often the norm.

Even if you are sold on the importance of having a public relations specialist on board, how do you sell the concept to your manager or to the budget office? Certainly, you don't want to try to convince them that financial commitment for public relations will help you get more money for the budget or garner more political support for the library! However, you can and should let your boss know that to invest hundreds of thousands or millions of dollars in library services and then withhold the relatively small amount it would cost to market those services is penny wise and pound foolish. And nothing could be truer. Is there a retailer anywhere that spends millions of dollars on inventory and then does nothing to promote it? Of course not, and the library (or the city, school, or university) shouldn't either.

If times are tight for the library, that's when you need a public relations specialist the most. In making the case for your library, you should make the case for funding public relations—or communications—or marketing. Your work in developing a good strong message for your library and sharing it with those who can influence the library's future will be significantly limited in its effect without a solid public relations effort to incorporate that message in all the ways previously discussed. Part of what makes a message effective is that it is consistent and omnipresent in all of your promotions. A piecemeal or part-time approach to public relations will get you piecemeal results. In addition, public relations is a professional discipline that few librarians have expertise for "on the side."

A library communications or public relations specialist can be the point person with the media, the one working to create speaking opportunities for you, your staff, and your trustees. This person will ensure that the message is conveyed in all your communications and promotions and can help design a consistent "look" for your library so that your promotional materials are immediately recognizable. The public relations specialist can create strong ties with fellow public relations people in your local media and may be able to get library coverage through these venues better than anyone else. In addition, your public relations specialist can work with the communications department of your larger organization, promoting the library through them and finding out for you what issues are "hot" and important to your administration at the moment.

Some institutions, cities, and organizations will recommend that the library rely for library promotions on an existing, centralized communications department. Resist the offer. The time it takes to continuously "educate" these off-site staff members will be staggering. And sadly, experience has shown many that libraries are at the bottom of their list of priorities, meaning that library press releases, newsletters, and the like will often be late or nonexistent when communication needs of the administration take precedence. The very fact that libraries get little respect in the larger organization's communication department just shows why you need your own person, in-house.

Fight hard for the staffing necessary to promote your library and its services. You may be able to leverage this by promising that if your organization will fund the staff, your Friends will support the costs for supplies and postage. Whatever it takes, think hard about ways to institutionalize public relations for your library so that your ongoing efforts to promote the library are professional and comprehensive.

4 CREATING SUCCESSFUL SLIDE OR POWERPOINT PRESENTATIONS

Developing a slide or PowerPoint presentation is a very effective way to increase the comfort level for those who are not natural public speakers and to ensure that the library's message is clear and consistent. In addition, having a presentation "in the can" will make it easier for you to say "yes" when invited to speak to organizations and groups, because you won't have to spend hours preparing for each occasion and you can develop a corps of trained library speakers. Finally, because making the presentation is so easy, a prepared presentation will facilitate your own efforts to reach out to the administration, local governments, agencies, and organizations.

This chapter provides guidance in developing and delivering an effective visual presentation for libraries of all types so that taking the library's message on the road will become part of your ongoing promotional campaign.

WHY A VISUAL PRESENTATION?

Slide and PowerPoint presentations are easy to develop and, importantly, easy to deliver. Significantly, such presentations do not require a great deal of expertise and financial resources to develop. Slide or PowerPoint presentations can be effective for both large and small groups and they are "portable" because you can bring your own equipment if a projector or computer isn't available at your destination. In addition, slide and PowerPoint presentations allow the presenter to narrate and add personal touches. The person presenting is able to "talk" to the audience rather than "read" from a prepared script. And, of course, it is often true that a picture—or graph or diagram—is worth a thousand words (your audience will thank you for making the exchange!).

Whether "low-tech" slides or high-tech PowerPoint, it's the content that counts, and your compelling message along with your creative talent can make a visual presentation as effective and interesting as any other method of presenting.

ARTICULATE THE DESIRED OUTCOME

As with all planning, the best place to start is at the end! What exactly do you hope to achieve from your efforts? Having the desired outcome clearly in mind will keep you focused as you make decisions regarding the content and use of your presentation.

Are you simply planning to tout your services to those who will be using them? If so, the approach you use will differ significantly from an approach designed to show those who fund you or who can influence funding why full support of the library matters. Certainly the latter approach is a much more effective advocacy tool. In fact, the desired outcome may be simply stated: "This presentation will convince the audience that library services are critical to the well being of our community, school, and/or institution and *must* be fully funded."

IDENTIFY YOUR PRIMARY AUDIENCE

Once your desired outcome has been articulated, it becomes easier to determine just whom you wish to persuade. In all likelihood, the intended audience will not necessarily be made up of strong library users. Your patrons already know the value of libraries. This presentation will not be designed to tell them more about what they already know, although the presentation should have the effect of convincing them to be more outspoken in their support of your library's services.

The *primary* audience is more likely to include infrequent library users and nonusers—those people who would be less inclined actively to support full funding of library services because they don't appreciate what's in it for them. If you have adopted a desired outcome similar to that stated above, you will not be focused on making users out of nonusers (although that may well be a favorable consequence).

The focus is to make your audience understand the value of your library's services and become active supporters whether they use them or not! This may not be as overwhelming a task as it may first appear. After all, we know that everyone benefits from a well-informed, well-educated community. We know that schools, colleges, and institutions are as strong as the information and learning resources they can provide their students and staff. The trick is to translate this view into terms that your audience can appreciate.

MAKE YOUR MESSAGE COUNT

If you have decided that your goal is to convince those who fund you and those who influence the funders that libraries matter and deserve full financial support, and if you have determined that those in positions of influence are not necessarily library users, then you have important information about how to shape your message.

In delivering your message it will be important to determine just what *does* matter to your audience and how library services impact their priorities. Consider these points for various types of libraries:

ACADEMIC LIBRARIES

- Curricular support
- Support for faculty research
- Support for students' independent learning
- "Bragging rights" for the parent institution's financial/endowment development

PUBLIC LIBRARIES

- Community pride
- Quality of life as it relates to community growth and development
- Lifelong learning opportunities for all community members
- Value—through free services
- Expansion of educational services for children

SCHOOL LIBRARIES

- Curricular support
- Hands-on education about and experience with the emerging electronic information infrastructure
- Value—through resource sharing
- Achievement of state educational standards
- Enhanced and expanded education for children
- Support for students' independent learning

SPECIAL LIBRARIES

- The competitive edge in the information age
- Value—through professional mediation and information retrieval
- Ongoing opportunity for staff development and education

MAXIMIZE THE EFFECTIVENESS OF THE MESSAGE

Knowing who your audience is, what their priorities are, and what you want to tell them will help you make your message as powerful as possible. It will be important to speak about what's important to them and how libraries play a role in their own priorities. As you develop your presentation be sure to focus on the issues that are important to your audience. For example, if your audience cares about marketing the college to new students, show how the library's state-of-the-art technology sets the college apart, let them know how increased funding can enhance what you are already providing and can attract the best and the brightest from the nation's high schools.

To be effective, your message must be simple and memorable. Keep the verbiage brief and the tone conversational. As always, let your own passion for the message come across to your audience. Because this is a visual presentation, show images that provide a strong human interest component. Slides and pictures showing the library being used by diverse users can be powerful, especially if one or more of these users illustrated is a recognizable VIP on campus or in the community.

Provide quotes and statistics that are clear and memorable. Charts and graphs that compare your statistics with others in the community or across the country can be more effective than citing a long list of use or resource figures. Quotes from community or campus leaders can be effective as can pertinent quotes from nationally known celebrities or leaders. The goal is to ensure that your audience will remember your key points long after the presentation is over. Strong images can help cement your message in their minds.

PUTTING A VISUAL PRESENTATION TOGETHER

Once you have done the foundational work of deciding what your message is and who will hear it, it is time to get down to the details of production. To organize the presentation you may want to create a storyboard. A storyboard is, quite simply, a plan for the development of the visual component of your presentation. This tool will help you create and lay out a logical sequence to the images you present and allow you to develop the supporting narrative to send the message in the most clear and cohesive way possible.

If you keep in mind the message you want to send and remember that you want to focus on your audience's priorities, you can develop a storyboard that includes pictures and graphs that will impress them as important aspects of your library's services. For example, for a presentation to civic organizations concerned with quality of life and community pride, a public library might want to include photos of the heavy use of the library, the high-tech or "glitzy" services, people using business resources, the diversity of materials available.

In addition, if you are trying to appeal to an audience that cares about quality of life because it fosters economic growth and development, for example, you may want to include charts and graphs showing how well your library stacks up with others in the state and nation. You may also want to include quotes that will be impressive—someone your audience respects linking libraries with progress, for example. It is important to remember—whether public, school, academic, or special library—to "spin" your message in accordance with your desired outcome *and* what you have identified as the audience's priorities.

When you have decided what images will best support your message, write what each image will be on a 3" x 5" notecard (one image per card). These cards can be arranged and rearranged until you feel you have a strong visual presentation that logically makes your case and will be remembered. Following are some tips for putting together a successful slide or PowerPoint presentation.

CREATING THE IMAGES

As important as the content of your message is, it is equally important that the quality of your presentation be top-notch. This presentation will be a direct reflection on the library; you want to be sure that it looks as professional as you would like your services to be viewed. Looking professional, however, does not mean you will have to spend a great deal of money to hire a professional photographer and graphic artist.

There are many books and articles to guide you in taking excellent photographs to enhance your message. In all likelihood, you will have someone among your staff, board of trustees, Friends, faculty, or students who is a very good amateur or even professional photographer who will give time and expertise to the library. It is important that you be very clear about the images you want to capture and that you request a generous number of photos be taken for each storyboard image.

You will increase the visual interest of your presentation if, in addition to photos, you include some graphs, quotes, and/or graphics. These enhancements can be generated on a variety of computer software and transferred to slides or moved into a PowerPoint presentation. The most important thing to remember in selecting your images is that they send the message you want and that they look professional.

DEVELOPING A SCRIPT OR NARRATIVE OUTLINE

There are two ways to approach the script or narrative for your presentation. The first is to audiotape the presentation so that it is literally self-explanatory. The other way is to develop an outline of key points to be made for each image and to allow the presenter to talk about the images as they come up.

Unless you are creating a slide-tape show or an audio-enhanced PowerPoint presentation that is to run and rerun automatically with no presenter on hand, you can get much more mileage out of a personally narrated presentation. Requiring that someone talk along with the slides lends a real human touch, gives you the opportunity to "personalize" your library to the audience, and engages the audience in a follow-up discussion much more readily. Truly, there is nothing like a library representative talking to an audience to increase audience interest and involvement in your presentation.

To develop an outline for the presenter, you will go back to your storyboard. All you need to do is support each image you've selected. The picture (or graph) will tell a lot of the story; the presenter's job is simply to fill in. Because you want the message you send to be both accurate and consistent, it is a good idea to ensure that the outline states clearly all statistics and facts presented and cites their source. Once you have connected the words with the pictures, you will need to spend time with everyone who will be a presenter and work with them so they are comfortable "fleshing out" the presentation.

Each image should be given a corresponding written idea or statement along with ideas for "filler information" that the presenter can include. For example, you may wish to start the presentation with a photo of your busy library, with the corresponding script "Over 1,000 students use our library every day." The narrator can then fill in with the important ways in which students are using the library to be successful in the classroom. The next image might be that of a student using the computer, with the corresponding script saying something like "In addition to using material available in the library, students can access information in databases across the country and across the globe." The filler information can then focus on how technology is changing the way we do business and how important it will be for graduates to be techno-savvy in order to be successful. These images might then be followed by a graph showing the numbers of jobs that require technology skills today versus those that did just 20 years ago. This graph could be followed effectively with such a statement as "Our library has played a leadership role on campus by providing access to electronic information and in teaching students about the information technology that is changing our world."

An effective script need not be lengthy or complex. In fact, the presentation will be strongest when the images can speak, in large part, for themselves. The idea is simply to expand on the photos and graphs to make them more memorable for the audience. Also, brief explanations of the images will help to invite questions from the audience at the end of the slide presentation.

TRAINING THE PRESENTERS

Now you have it—a slide presentation that sends the message you want to send. It's professional and persuasive. Time to take a break? Not yet. Although much of the detail work has been completed, you have two more important tasks ahead of you. The first is to train those who will be presenting the slide show and the second is to line up engagements to take your show on the road!

Before you begin the training, you should determine just who you would like to represent the library. Certainly there will be staff members who can represent the library well, but you may gain some political advantage if you have a cadre of presenters outside the library as well. A list of potential presenters might include:

- President of the Friends of the Library
- Members of the Board of Trustees or the advisory council
- Department heads
- Supportive (and articulate) patrons
- Students

Once you have identified and received a positive response from a potential pool of presenters, the most effective training technique might well be to bring them together for the "premier showing" of the slide presentation. This is the perfect time to evaluate the presentation. Does the message you want to send come through? Don't hesitate to make recommended changes, even at this point, to ensure that your desired outcome will be realized. You've put a lot of work into the production thus far; a little more modification to strengthen the presentation is worth it.

Bringing the group together now will also give you an opportunity to ensure that the message you wish to send is consistent among those delivering it. In addition, it is an opportunity to brainstorm ways to "fill out" the statements that support the images.

Because the presentation is narrated, each presenter can personalize the presentation, and, because you don't require (or want!) lengthy discourse, even those with very limited public speaking experience will be comfortable. Make enough copies of the outline (which should include a brief description of each image along with the corresponding statement) so presenters can become familiar with the script before going before an audience. Review the presentation several times, giving each potential presenter a chance to practice in front of the group for at least a couple of slides.

<u>NOTE</u>: This is a good time to make sure all presenters know the rudiments of the slide projector or laptop computer!

TAKING THE SHOW ON THE ROAD

The slide show is ready, the presenters are trained. There's only one thing left to do . . . line up the audience! While it's true that often groups and organizations will come to you, you've put a lot of time and effort into this project, so it makes sense to get as much mileage out of it as possible.

What audience have you identified? Don't wait for them to ask you what you're up to, now is the time to get in touch with them and let them know you have information to share about the library. Although you have put a "spin" on the program in order to influence a particular group (the school administration or city council for example), realize that many in your community, school, or on your campus can indirectly influence the policy makers as well. Determine who these groups are and make a comprehensive list. They might include:

- Administrators
- Local government leaders
- Civic leaders
- Alumni associations
- Faculty
- Civic organizations
- Media organizations
- Trustees
- Student organizations
- Chamber of Commerce

The list of prospective audience groups should be as long as you can make it. Saturate the market! Make sure everyone who has a stake in your library and/or the ability to affect its future has an opportunity to see this presentation.

Once you have developed a list, begin to make contacts. Matching the presenter with the group may end up being a matter of expediency—who's available when the group or organization is able to put you on their agenda. If you have some discretion, however, you can gain even more ground by matching the presenter with the organization. The children's librarian might be the most effective presenter to the PTA, for example, while the library director should be the one who presents to the city council or academic administration.

Gaining the opportunity to present will be easier than you think, and, if you've done a good job, you are likely to receive calls from other groups and organizations who have heard about the presentation and would like to see it too.

By the end of the year, you'll see your efforts have paid off with a constituency that is better informed about what the library has to offer and why it matters!

CHECKLIST FOR SLIDE OR POWERPOINT PRESENTATIONS

- ➤ Articulate the desired outcome. What message do you want your audience to take from the presentation?
- ➤ Know your audience. What are their concerns/priorities and how does the library fit in?
- ➤ Make the message count. Match your desired outcome with your audience's concerns and priorities.
- ➤ Create images. Select and arrange messages that support your message.
- ➤ Outline the script. Outline a script that emphasizes key issues and is designed to persuade.
- ➤ Evaluate the finished product. Does the finished product clearly and powerfully reflect the desired outcome?
- ➤ Train the staff. Determine who should represent the library and give the presenters an opportunity to practice.
- ➤ Take the show on the road. Don't be shy; contact the groups who have influence in the funding decisions affecting your library and make a date to take your slide-show on the road.

PART III
TARGETING THE MESSAGE

5 PRODUCING THE TARGETED CAMPAIGN

Effectively producing a targeted campaign with a very specific goal requires:

- Planning
- Enlarging the circle of library supporters
- Effective use of grassroots support
- Effective advertising campaigns
- Effective use of the media
- Follow-up and evaluation

From time to time, it will be necessary for your trustees and Friends to wage a very special, targeted campaign. Whether you are making the case for a significant budget increase, warding off proposed budget cuts, or working to get approval for a major capital campaign, there will come a time when you will need to generate solid and overwhelming support for your library for a specific purpose. This is when all you've done to educate the leaders in your organization about the importance of libraries pays off. This is when you will be especially thankful that you've got an active Friends group and an influential Board of Trustees. This is your opportunity to see how laying the groundwork through ongoing advocacy can make a real difference when the need is great and the chips are down.

Implementing a special advocacy campaign for a specific targeted purpose takes careful and thoughtful planning. While you will probably be instrumental in getting the planning for a campaign off the ground, it's important for you to stay in the background and let those who have influence or who can influence others do the talking. Your job in the initial stages of this campaign will be to inform your library support groups of the need (new building, significant funding increase, or the like), let them know the time frame for implementation, and work with them in identifying strategies and avenues for making the case.

PLANNING

As with all successful planning, the best place to begin is at the end. What is the desired outcome of this campaign? Are you working toward a significant budget increase? Are you trying to pass a referendum? Are you working to forestall a policy that could hurt the library? Identify clearly and concisely what your goal is and then work back from there. To begin planning strategy for a targeted campaign, it is best to start with a small group of library supporters (the trustees or the Friends executive board would be ideal) and figure out what must happen to get what the library needs.

If you are seeking a significant budget increase (or warding off a cut), you will have to establish who can make a difference for the library's budget. Who makes the ultimate decision? How do they make it? For example, in a city the budget may be ultimately passed by the city council, but do they generally rubber-stamp the city manager's proposal? If so, then the key person to influence may be the city manager. If the city council is known for overriding the manager's recommendation, you may have better success in influencing the council.

It is important to identify who has the most power in this scenario because it will definitely affect your approach. If the city manager, for example, always has the last word, then a grassroots campaign *may* not be as effective as a full-court press by the Board of Trustees or other persons of influence in your city. In this case, you may want your trustees to set up an appointment with the manager to discuss their concerns about the library. They might want to take a petition signed by hundreds in the city supporting the proposed increase. It will be important to know the city manager and understand what arguments tend to work best with him or her. Truthfully, it is often more difficult to influence one person who is not worried about reelection than to deal with a group like the city council that is easily swayed by public opinion.

If, for example, you are working to ensure the passage of a public referendum or bond issue for the library, then your ultimate target audience is the voting public. Understanding that it is the grass roots you are trying to influence will help you focus your efforts on persuading them to vote in the library's favor. Knowing the public and the prevailing public sentiment is important and should be discussed, because the campaign you wage must address their concerns in a way that influences their positive support. If cutting taxes at all costs is a high priority, then you should make the case that your library can save individuals money. Compare the increase in tax dollars per capita for the library to the cost of buying a book. Use favorite bumper sticker slogans such as "Libraries will get you through times of no money better than money will get you through times of no libraries." Talk about libraries as an investment. Be sure to underscore the broad base of use your library gets and the small portion of the overall institutional budget that's dedicated to the library.

In the planning process, with a small leadership group, you will want to identify the person or group that will make the ultimate decision regarding the library's future, what matters most to the decision makers, and what (or who) will have the most influence over them. Once you've established this, the working group should develop some ideas for action and set up a time line for implementing the action plan.

EXPANDING THE CIRCLE

Once a tentative plan is drawn up, it is important for the working group to enlarge the circle of campaign volunteers. This expansion is important for two reasons. First of all, you will get a lot more creative thinking with a larger group, and you can incorporate that into an action plan. Second, you need as many people as possible on board from the beginning if you are waging a grassroots campaign. The more people who are involved in the planning stage, the more actively committed people you'll have who clearly understand the issues from the beginning and can help deliver the message.

Be sure that in working with this group, a time line for action is drawn up and assignments are clear. In delegating responsibility for various tasks, be crystal clear about what is expected and when the task should be completed. The initial working group should assume management of the overall process and someone should take on the leadership role. This campaign leader needs to keep track of who has been assigned what task and then the leader must call each volunteer at various points through the process to be sure that tasks are being accomplished and deadlines are being met.

THE CAMPAIGN BEGINS

If you need large numbers to influence the decision makers or to pass a vote, it is time to put the power of your constituents to work. No matter what environment your library operates in—city, town, school, academic, or corporate—you have a constituency. At the very least, you have your users. In most cases, however, libraries have an even broader base from which to draw. Public libraries have the business community and even supportive nonusers. Schools, colleges, and universities have parents (never underestimate the power of those who are paying the bills). The academic community also has alumni, Friends groups (that may consist of faculty members, alumni, and local business people), and students to draw upon for support. It's pretty easy to identify the supporters in your community; the trick is to turn passive support into active support to help make the case for your library.

For most grassroots campaigns, the goal is sheer numbers. Sheer numbers will pass the vote and sheer numbers can influence decision makers on behalf of your library. This doesn't mean, in the case of increased funding, that you and your key supporters need not continue to work one-on-one with the decision makers (and aim to get those who have influence over the decision makers to work on the library's behalf as well). It's just that, in the case of a public vote or in the case of reluctant councils or administrators, a public campaign can finally tip the balance for the library.

THE "VOTE YES" CAMPAIGN

Do you want a "yes" vote? Then your message is simple. A "Vote Yes" campaign will have a clear deadline and the campaign committee will be able to work backward from the day of the vote to begin to wage the campaign. A vote or referendum will require as much an education campaign as it will a campaign to get supporters out to vote. While almost everyone likes and respects libraries, not everyone wants to pay for them (or pay more for them).

The message about the library's importance to everyone, even to those who do not use the library, will be critical. Everyone who votes, or who is likely to vote, will have to understand what is in it for him or her—or what is in it for someone they care about, such as their grandchildren or their home-bound aunt. Not only will voters need to be convinced that the library can make a difference in their lives, but they will have to be convinced that the library is worth paying for.

The library's Friends group should be instrumental in securing a positive vote for the library. To begin with, a broad-based campaign will probably be expensive if it's to be effective. In addition, there will be a lot of work to do, and the more people you have involved the more penetrating and visible the campaign will be. Some of the tools to consider using to get a supportive vote for the library are:

- Letters to the editor
- Ad campaigns
- Flyer or postcard campaign
- Telephone campaign

LETTERS TO THE EDITOR AND NEWSPAPER SUPPORT

Before you begin your full-court press to target specific library supporters for the vote or to urge specific action, it's a good idea to begin a more broad-based campaign using the local media—particularly the local paper. If there is to be a major referendum for library funding or an aggressive campaign for increased funding, it's likely that your local newspaper has already begun to cover the issue. You can increase support for your cause if you can persuade the paper to write an editorial in favor of the library.

If someone among the library support groups has connections with the paper's editorial staff, use that connection. The paper will be interested in talking to someone (probably from the library's trustees or Friends) who can express the inside perspective on why the library needs additional funding or building. There's no guarantee that you'll be able to persuade the paper to take a stand on your behalf, but it won't hurt to try to get editorial support.

If you can't get an editorial, or even if you can, try to secure space for an op-ed piece. The president of the Board of Trustees would be the perfect person to make the library's case in an op-ed column. If you can get a promise for this space, be sure that the article doesn't speak to the choir. Instead imagine the audience as those who sit on the fence. What are the concerns? What are the objections? Anticipate why people might be reluctant to vote for the library's plan and answer those concerns. Make sure the op-ed piece is well written, compelling, and gets the key message across to the reader. Figure 3.13 is a good example.

Letters to the editor can also be influential. The more letters you are able to submit, the more will be printed. Even four or five letters to the editor can begin to look like a groundswell movement. It is unlikely that your paper will print hundreds of letters supporting the library, but you may need to try to get hundreds sent in so that you create what looks like a major trend of support. In fact, the more letters to the editor you are able to generate, the higher the likelihood that the newspaper's staff will consider writing an editorial in the library's favor.

Someone from the volunteer committee should be assigned the task of getting letters to the editor generated and sent. A small task force for this purpose would be a good idea. Even the best supporters may be reluctant to write, so the task force has to identify potential letter writers, contact these people and convince them to commit, and develop a list of key points that the letter writers can use. The easier you make it for the letter writers, the more likely they are to follow through. Some campaigns actually give letter writers a sample letter, but the potential downside is that they will not modify the letter enough and the paper will get multiple form letters. In that case, they are likely to print only one. It's best to give your letter writers the address of the paper, the format they should use, a list of key points, a request that they add their personal reason for supporting the library, and a deadline. Once the writers have all the information they need, it's a good idea to follow up in a week or two to see if they've written the letter or to give them some more encouragement if they haven't. Figures 5.1 and 5.2, sample letters in support of a capital campaign, show why the vote matters and what is in it for the community.

SAMPLE LETTER TO THE EDITOR

[Capital Campaign, Public Library]

To the Editor:

It is estimated that 80% of incarcerated Americans are functionally illiterate. Furthermore, it costs an average of $20,000 per year to keep one individual behind bars. Compare that to the cost of supporting our Anytown Public Library's plan for rebuilding its system. If the upcoming bond referendum is passed, citizens of this community will pay approximately $40 per year for the next 20 years to keep our library system healthy, attractive, usable, and up-to-date. This is a system that provides services to over 250,000 people from all walks of life, ensuring that they have access to the information and materials they need to be fully literate and to contribute positively to our community.

The connection between crime and illiteracy is crystal clear while the cost of supporting life-long literacy through libraries is downright cheap. The time has come for all of us in Anytown to support the library's efforts to rebuild a crumbling and inadequate infrastructure. Our library buildings are old and down at the heels. Not a single library in our system has adequate space or wiring to provide the best in the new information technology. As our city has grown and as library use continues to rise, it is time to reinvest in this most important crime prevention institution – the public library.

I urge all library users – and all who care about crime prevention – to support the Anytown library in its bid for rebuilding. Please vote "yes" on October 14.

Sincerely yours,

John Q. Public

Figure 5.1—Sample letter to the editor (capital campaign).

This letter to the editor points out the link between illiteracy and crime (and issue for many city governments) and shows that libraries are part of the solution. Building libraries is cheaper and more productive than building prisons.

SAMPLE LETTER TO THE EDITOR
[Capital Campaign Letter]

Dear Editor:

On November 12, we the citizens of Anycity will have an opportunity to dramatically improve the quality of life for ourselves, our children and generations yet to come. On November 12, we can vote "yes" for a new central library.

Why now, why at all? Our central library was built 45 years ago and has not been remodeled or expanded since. In that same time period, however, our city has grown 100% and the number of registered patrons of the library has increased 150%. In addition to being too small to accommodate the growth in use, our library was not built to handle the new information technology that has become such a critical part of public library service. Here's what a new library will provide for you (and your grandchildren!):

- State of the art technology lab for public use and public instruction
- Three meeting rooms for public use
- A Children's Room twice the size of our current room with abundant collections for kids aged 0-12
- A new Teen Center to encourage kids 13-18 to use the library and indulge in the joys of reading
- Expanded reference services delivered on location, online, and over the phone
- Spacious accommodation for our outstanding collection of fiction and nonfiction and plenty of room for this well-used collection to grow
- A new local history room with space for display and easy access to materials central to our local history, and online virtual access to diaries, letters, posters, playbills and other ephemera that has required special handling and thus has limited our access

What a gift a great public library is – to all of us. Let's give ourselves this gift on November 12 and leave behind a legacy that will make future generations proud.

Sincerely,

Mary C. Citizen

Figure 5.2—Sample letter to the editor (capital campaign).

This letter knows its audience and clearly spells out what a new building will mean to the taxpayer / voter.

ADVERTISING CAMPAIGNS

Advertising campaigns cost money—both to develop the ads and to purchase the airtime or space to disseminate them. It's not too likely that you'll get free space or air for a direct political ad, so you'll want to be sure that funding for paid advertising is included in your budget. In addition, unless you have access to someone with marketing expertise, you will need to hire professionals to help you develop a campaign—and it will be money well spent. Professionals can help you use the right medium to target the right target audience. They will help you shape your message in a way that works for the desired audience. In the ideal situation, if you are going to spend money on newspaper, radio, or television ads, you want to be sure that someone can analyze the demographics and help you position your ad campaign in the most advantageous way. It may be hard to come up with the funding, but spending some money here can save you from wasting it on an expensive ad campaign in the wrong paper, on the wrong days, targeting the wrong audience.

If you are not able to obtain the professional public relations services, you still should be able to get professional advice and assistance. Many newspapers and television and radio stations have marketing personnel who will help you design an ad as part of the service you get for placing one. Talk to their advertising departments to find out when you can get the most bang for your buck. You may save money by purchasing a half-page layout on a strategically important day of week (the day before the vote, for example) versus buying a full-page display on a Saturday when readership is traditionally lower and people's minds may not be on civic or political matters. Radio stations can tell you when you can capture your audience at the most cost-effective time.

Be sure that the newspaper ad your support committee designs is bold and eye catching but also make sure that the message is compelling. Radio announcements should also be catchy and in a short period of time they should let the listener know what to do (vote for the library) and why it matters. Why should your citizens vote "yes"? You may want to get the permission of leading citizens to use their names in the advertisement as endorsing the vote. Finally, make sure that any advertisement purchased to support the library is clearly marked with the tag line "Paid for by the Friends of the Anytown Public Library." You don't want either your administration or your voters to assume that tax money is being spent on a political campaign.

FLYERS AND POSTCARDS

A mass mailing can be expensive, but done judiciously, it can really pay off in terms of making sure that known library supporters get out to vote. By using the Friends mailing list, and any other list that has been generated of known or potential library supporters (such as library foundation members, civic league officers, and local educators), you can send a flyer or postcard shortly before the vote letting them know that their "yes" vote counts. In addition, ask them to contact at least three friends or relatives to get additional support and votes for the library.

Again, it is important to let those on your mailing list know *why* the library needs their support. Just because someone gave $10 to join the Friends doesn't mean they'll vote "yes" for a $50 million bond issue. Don't take them for granted, let them know why it matters and what's in it for them. Give them the ammunition they need to make the library's case with their own friends and colleagues.

Finally, be sure to include the voting date on your postcard or flyer. Everything you can do to make it easy for them to get out and vote for the library should be included. I have heard many librarians conclude, when analyzing a failed bond vote or referendum, that too many supporters just never got around to voting.

Figures 5.3–5.5 are examples of effective promotional handouts.

A NEW LIBRARY

Long Overdue!

Figure 5.3a—Brochure for building, Suffern (N.Y.) Free Library.

This inexpensive brochure shows clearly that a new library is an excellent investment and gives clear instructions to the voter.

WHY DO WE NEED A NEW LIBRARY IN WEST RAMAPO?

Simply put, Suffern Library has no more room - no more room for books, for patrons to sit, for computers, tables, added story hours, or parking. We've reached the limit. And the current 7,359 sq. ft. building on a 120' x 200' site can't be expanded because of surrounding private housing.

The Library's service area covers 25,963 people in 6 villages in West Ramapo: Suffern, Montebello, Hillburn, Sloatsburg,* most of Airmont, a small part of Wesley Hills, and a portion of unincorporated Ramapo. This is the fourth largest library district in the County. But the Library is one of the smallest. The residents of the district deserve better!

WHERE WILL THE NEW LIBRARY BE?

on a six acre partially wooded lot, located on the north side of Route 59, adjacent to the Tagaste Monastery.

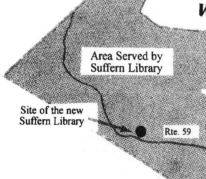

Area Served by Suffern Library

Site of the new Suffern Library

Rte. 59

WHY WAS THIS SITE CHOSEN?

It was selected because it is:

- located in the population center of Western Ramapo
- accessible by public transportation
- large enough to accommodate the library's needs for the next 50 years.

WHAT SIZE WILL THE LIBRARY BE? After working with a library building consultant, architects, and engineering firms, the Trustees determined that a building between 37,000 and 39,000 square feet was needed to provide library services for the next 20 years.

HOW MUCH WILL IT COST? The architectural and engineering consultants have estimated that the project cost, including land, furnishings, and site costs will not exceed $7.3 million,

WHAT WILL BE DONE WITH THE OLD BUILDING? It will be sold and the proceeds will be applied to costs associated with the new library.

* (also served by the Sloatsburg Village Library)

Figure 5.3b—Brochure for building, Suffern (N.Y.) Free Library.

This inexpensive brochure shows clearly that a new library is an excellent investment and gives clear instructions to the voter.

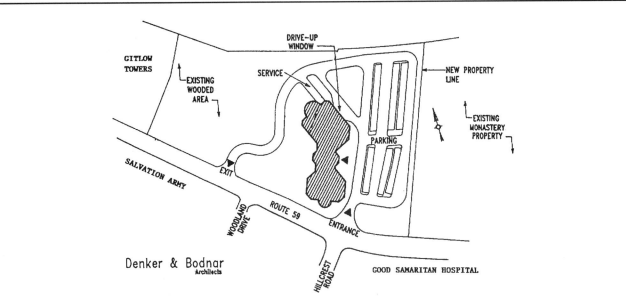

Conceptual drawing of the building on the Rte. 59 site

WHAT WOULD BE IN THE NEW LIBRARY?

The Board believes the library should be a true community center. Some of the likely features are:

- shelving for 150,000 books (library currently has 75,000 books)
- a separate children's story time/craft room for programs
- a larger new book and browsing area
- seating of all types (from 74 seats in the current library to 172)
- local history room
- meeting room space
- parking for over 100 cars

- handicapped accessibility
- wiring for technology with plenty of room for computers
- an audio visual area with videos, CD's on open browsing shelves
- drive-in return and pick up window
- quiet study spaces
- art exhibit area
- small meeting rooms
- coffee bar, if community response is positive.

CAN WE SEE ARCHITECTURAL PLANS?

At this point there are conceptual drawings of the building and its placement on the site. These can be viewed at the library. An architect for the actual design and specifications will not be hired until the community approves the funding. At that time various options for the interior space will be developed with the help of the community.

Figure 5.3c—Brochure for building, Suffern (N.Y.) Free Library.

This inexpensive brochure shows clearly that a new library is an excellent investment and gives clear instructions to the voter.

FACTS FOR VOTERS

WHEN: **THURSDAY, APRIL 17TH, 1997**

POLLS OPEN: 7 am to 9 pm

WHO: Residents of the Ramapo Central School District who are registered to vote in a general or school district election.

WHERE: Five Polling Places:

Cherry Lane School   Suffern Middle School
R. P. Connor School   Sloatsburg School
Hillburn Administration Building.

REGISTRATION:

Tuesday, April 8th, 1 pm - 8 pm at same polling places as above. You must be a school district resident for 30 days, and a US citizen 18 years or older.

INFORMATION MEETING: APRIL 3rd at 8 pm at Suffern Library.

NEED AN ABSENTEE BALLOT?
Call 357-1237 - Library
357-7783 - School office

Figure 5.3d—Brochure for building, Suffern (N.Y.) Free Library.

This inexpensive brochure shows clearly that a new library is an excellent investment and gives clear instructions to the voter.

HOW WILL THE LIBRARY BE PAID FOR?

The Suffern Library does not have authority to issue bonds. A mortgage is the usual method of financing construction. However, the State Dormitory Authority is now able to issue bonds on behalf of designated libraries. Their financing would allow us to spread the entire cost over 30 years and their bonds are nontaxable. By acting now and taking advantage of this opportunity, library taxpayers could save approximately $141,000 in interest per year, compared to financing with a mortgage.

THE BOTTOM LINE FOR TAXPAYERS

The money needed to pay interest and principal on Dormitory Authority bonds for the new library requires an increase in the community's annual tax support for the library of $590,000.

That's what the voters are being asked to approve on Thursday, April 17th. The Table below shows the increase in library property tax for homes or condominiums with different assessments.

ASSESSED VALUE	MARKET VALUE	TAX INCREASE
$ 40,000	$ 128,493	$ 38.00
$ 50,000	$ 160,616	$ 47.50
$ 70,000	$ 224,863	$ 66.50
$100,000	$ 321,233	$ 95.00

DIDN'T THE VOTERS ALREADY APPROVE FUNDS FOR EXPANSION?

Yes. The capital increase approved in 1995 for the first steps for expansion is being applied to planning, downpayment on land purchase, preliminary site planning including engineering costs, appraisals, library and architectural consultants, and similar expenses.

WILL THERE BE PRIVATE FUND RAISING?

Yes. There will be a fund raising campaign. Opportunities will be available for gifts for special purposes in honor of individuals, or in memory of a loved one.

Figure 5.3e—Brochure for building, Suffern (N.Y.) Free Library.

This inexpensive brochure shows clearly that a new library is an excellent investment and gives clear instructions to the voter.

LIBRARY
BUILDING PROGRAM

| FOREST | $2,400,000 |
| 10,000 SQUARE FEET | |

| MONETA | $2,400,000 |
| 10,000 SQUARE FEET | |

| STEWARTSVILLE | $1,000,000 |
| 3,000 SQUARE FEET | |

| MONTVALE | $1,000,000 |
| 3,000 SQUARE FEET | |

| BIG ISLAND | $ 200,000 |
| 750 SQUARE FOOT EXPANSION | |

| BOND COSTS | $ 100,000 |

$7,100,000

Published by
Bedford Public Library
Board of Trustees

Figure 5.4—Bookmark for building, Bedford (Va.) Public Library System.

Clear, concise information (especially noting when to vote) can be widely distributed to the library's best supporters—its users.

TOP TEN

Reasons to vote <u>YES</u> on Issue 32 for Southwest Public Libraries

<u>The Library Board of Trustees will:</u>

 1 Purchase more library materials such as books, videos and recordings.

 2 Implement new technological services.

 3 Make building and parking lot improvements.

 4 Increase Outreach visits to patrons who are unable to come to the library, such as nursing home residents, preschoolers, homebound residents and others.

 5 Establish public computer labs in both libraries.

 6 Install Discovery Place terminals in schools, senior centers and other locations to provide computer access to library resources.

 7 Increase library hours, including Sundays.

 8 Add a CD-ROM network for children.

 9 Expand family-oriented programs.

10 Add more staff to assist patrons.

Southwest Public Libraries... OVERDUE Vote *YES!* Nov. 5

Figure 5.5—Flyer for building, Southwest Public Libraries, Grove City, Ohio.

This attractive flyer is clear about what's in it for the community, what it will cost and what the citizens should do—Vote Yes!

TELEPHONE REMINDERS

Calling your known supporters (such as the Friends) can be a very time-consuming enterprise but it may be the most effective. The volunteer support group should plan to divide up whatever lists are available for library supporters and create a telephone tree. The night before the vote, an attempt to call everyone on your lists will go a long way to ensure that you don't lose votes simply because supporters didn't get around to voting or believed that the issue would pass without them.

Because cold calls are often difficult for even the staunchest library supporter to make, it will be important to take every hurdle you can out of the process. Develop a small task force from the volunteer committee to spend time, a couple weeks prior to the telephone campaign, getting current phone numbers for everyone on the list. In addition, write out a script so that volunteer callers will know exactly what to say. The script should be very short, very polite, and very clear that every vote is needed.

If the library's volunteer support committee has done its job well, there has already been plenty of publicity on the issue and everyone calling or being called has already received at least one written communiqué explaining exactly what the library is looking for and why. Therefore, to keep the calls extremely short and sweet, the script might be as simple as:

> My name is Jane Doe and I am working on behalf of the committee to support our public library. I am urging you to vote tomorrow and please to vote "yes." The polls are open from 9 a.m. to 8 p.m. Can we count on you?

This short script will be appreciated by the recipient and allow the caller to move quickly through his or her list.

It's likely that callers will get questions and objections even though you think you are calling supporters. It's a good idea to arm the callers with a fact sheet that explains what a "yes" vote will mean. Anticipate the questions a citizen may have and provide all the callers with a flyer that answers them. How much will this raise my taxes each year and for how long? When will building begin? Will the services I currently enjoy continue or will they change? How much will operating expenses increase with a new building? What new services will be available if this vote passes? It's also a good idea to include basic facts about current library services. How many residents use the library? In what ways is the library used? What is the ratio of adults to children in use? What is the current library budget?

The more you can provide your volunteer callers with information and assistance up front, the more likely they'll be to make their calls. Because calling is a hard job for some, it's best that you don't work to talk a reluctant volunteer into it. It's possible that someone who wasn't readily willing will agree to call just to avoid saying no. Better to have longer calling lists for willing volunteers than to have calls go unmade.

THE CAMPAIGN TO INFLUENCE DECISION MAKERS

When the ultimate decision regarding your library's future for funding, policy, or building lies with a governing body and not directly with the people, the grassroots campaign takes on a slightly different direction from one that is trying to influence a broad-based vote. Where a direct vote campaign is likely to be an option only for public libraries, a campaign to influence the decision makers is possible in any kind of library environment.

Efforts to influence decision makers can take on two forms. The first attempt should be to influence those in control directly. Work with leaders in your community or on campus who have special sway over those who will decide the library's fate. Working one-on-one with the administrators or council members who will decide the library's budget or its future plans can be effective. If you've done a good job in your ongoing advocacy campaign, it's very likely that you've been able to raise the collective consciousness of those in power regarding the importance of your library and its request.

A quiet campaign by community leaders to convince decision makers to support the library's agenda may be all that's needed. Identify those who have power on campus or in your community and work to sell them on the library's plans so they, in turn, can wield their influence. If you have influential members of the trustees or Friends, a few calls and personal visits from them to the powers that be may work for you. This is, of course, just where you want to be in terms of the library's perceived importance.

As always, help community leaders to make the case in terms of what's in it for the decision makers to support the library's request. "The library's good and important" just won't cut it in most cases. To be effective, the library's plans must be sold as a way of helping your administration and government achieve their goals. If increased enrollment is a goal, how will improving the library make a real difference in achieving that goal? If your community is concerned about increased crime rates, how does the library make a difference for public safety? Knowing what's important to your administration will help you make the case in the most politically powerful way possible—not by arguing what the library needs, but by showing how your plans for improved library services will help to meet *their* needs.

Despite all your good efforts to send a strong political message for your library in your long-term communication and marketing efforts, it may be that you and those who are leaders in your community just aren't able to sway the people making decisions about the library's future. When all else fails, it may be time to let the library's constituents do the talking.

Things have to get pretty bad before the rank and file see that the library is in dire need of improvements. More likely, as the professional you will know in advance what kind of support the library needs if it is to continue to deliver quality services in a changing environment. In the planning process it will be clear where the library should be heading and what it will take to get there. A good director will keep his or her administration, trustees, and Friends involved in the vision for the library and should educate these people about what it will take to realize the vision. When the time comes for a significant increase in support for the library, it should not be a surprise to the people closest to the library administration.

When funding support, building, or a change in policy becomes necessary, the trustees and Friends should be ready to make the case to the library's constituents if they have been unsuccessful in making that case to the decision makers. Now is the time to embark on a public awareness campaign designed to enlist the aid of the grassroots to pressure the organization's administration and governors into supporting the library.

In this kind of campaign, you ask library supporters to take action that shows the degree to which the community at large supports the library's plans for improvement. There are a variety of ways to do this creatively and effectively. It's important to note that this type of campaign takes as much thought and planning as one designed to get a direct public vote for the library.

Working backwards from a deadline, a committee of volunteer supporters, headed up by such a group as the trustees or Friends, should begin to brainstorm about ways to ensure that as many of your constituents as possible are counted as supporting the library's specific needs. Just as with a vote, numbers count. The more library supporters you can get to sign on as supporting your special library agenda, the more you will be able to influence the final decision makers to support the library's goals.

To be especially successful, some broad-based education about what the library is asking for and why will be necessary. Using the Friends newsletter, ads in the paper, op-ed opportunities, and flyers, the first thing the committee should do is spread the word about the library's plans in a general way. In addition to using the media, the core committee should begin networking with civic leagues, campus groups, and other community organizations. Assign everyone on the core committee to attend at least one meeting of an appropriate group on campus or in the community. Service groups, for example, are always interested in getting speakers and many in your library support groups will belong to such organizations or groups. Personal presentations about the library's needs and goals are excellent ways to begin to get the word out.

Be sure in assigning speaking engagements that volunteers are able to articulate what the library needs and why. In addition, they should be able to answer general questions about library services. All volunteers who are going to make the case for the library should understand how the library's plans will benefit the audience. It's important that anyone agreeing to speak on the library's behalf be fully prepared (see *Presentations* in Part II). Using some of the same techniques that are used in a "vote yes" campaign, the committee should plan for the public awareness campaign to precede any efforts to get constituent endorsement. In the best case, if the volunteer support committee is able to generate enough "buzz" about the library and the plans to reach out to the grass roots, the local media may take it on as newsworthy, giving this campaign even more visibility and momentum.

In addition to getting the word out about the library's plans in a general way, the committee will have to decide which strategies will be used to convey that the library's plans are fully supported by many in the community or on campus. A variety of devices will allow you to identify supporters and show that they have signed on in support. Some of the strategies may include:

- Letter-writing campaign
- Letter-to-the-editor campaign
- Petition drive
- Telephone-call campaign
- Postcard campaign
- E-mail campaign

Depending on the time frame, the level of commitment from the core volunteer committee, and the finances available, the library support committee can ask the grassroots to engage in any or all of these strategies. In the end, whatever strategies are used, your campaign has to let the grassroots know the following:

- Exactly what action you would like them to take (such as make a call, sign a petition, write a letter to the editor).

- How they can take that action. Where will they find a petition to sign? What phone number should they call? What key points should they include in a letter to the editor?
- Why they should take action. Even though you may have a large mailing list for the Friends of the Library don't assume that a simple request will get them all to act. Even supporters will want to know *why* they are being asked to act, what is at stake for library services.
- The deadline for action. This can be a little tricky. It takes time to activate a large grassroots campaign, but if you provide too big a time frame, procrastination will cause many to forget to act at all and it may spread action out to the degree that support appears to be "thinner" than it actually is.

LETTERS

A barrage of letters to the editor or directly to the decision makers can be highly effective (as it is with the "Vote Yes" campaign). It can be, however, the most difficult action to get hundreds of supporters to take. Therefore, a two-tiered approach here is probably best. The core campaign committee should identify a solid number of influential members of the community and ask them to write letters to the editor just prior to the kick-off of the grassroots campaign. This approach will have the dual effect of influencing the grassroots to take action when the time comes, and it will send a message to the decision makers that influential community or campus members care about the library.

Letters directly to the decision makers are also effective. Who writes those letters can be more important, however, than the number of letters actually sent. Determine which library supporters have influence with decision makers and ask those people to write a letter on your behalf. The Friends executive board members and the trustees should write, too, not only to ask for their support, but also to let them know that a grassroots campaign is being planned. This information isn't to threaten them but to give them a "heads up," so they are not blindsided by the press and so they are aware of how important your supporters believe this issue to be.

Both those writing letters to the editor and those writing directly to decision makers should be able to stay clearly on message while using their own voice to make the case. To ensure that their message is accurate and consistent, the core committee should draft a flyer of points that can be incorporated into the message. A list of points should include the following:

- Exactly what the library is seeking
- Why it matters
- What the consequences of unmet needs will be
- Any history or background pertinent to the request
- Specifically what action you would like the decision maker to take

Figure 5.6 is a good example of such a list.

What does the library need?
1% of the city's operating budget for Libraries.

What % does the Library receive now?
The Libraries currently receive 0.8%.

What does this mean in terms of dollars?
The Library's current operating budget of $4.8 million would be increased to about $6 million.

What % have the Libraries received in the past?
Historically, the city has funded libraries at or above 1% of its budget. From fiscal year 1980 through 1987 the library received more than 1.2% of the city's budget. This fell to approximately 1% in fiscal years 1988 through 1991. In fiscal year 1992 funding dropped below 1% and continued to drop to 0.76% in fiscal year 1996. With a few small increases the library now receives 0.8% of the city's budget.

What is the significance of the 1% level of funding?
The American Library Association acknowledges that 1% to 1.4% of a city budget is the traditional measure of adequate and appropriate funding for a major urban library.

What would 1% for Libraries provide?
With funding at the requested 1% level, the Libraries would enhance economic development and education while improving delivery of library services to all citizens.
♦ Improved book collections at all locations
♦ Fully staffed and equipped computer lab for public use at Kirn Memorial Library
♦ Fully staffed, full-time access to Kirn's Sargeant Memorial Room
♦ Fully staffed and equipped computer lab for public use at Park Place Branch Library (to continue previously grant-funded position)
♦ Additional Bookmobile service throughout the city through van service

What can you do to help?
One voice can make a difference. Please take one minute of your time today to make one phone call to the Office of the Mayor at 664-4679 and voice your support for 1% for Libraries.

Figure 5.6—Flyer to support operating budget, Norfolk (Va.) Public Library.

This flyer anticipates and answers questions citizens and campaign volunteers may have and gives clear direction on what a supporter can do to help.

PETITION DRIVES

Petition drives can be the easiest way to coalesce the support you have for a special request. Signing a petition requires a lot less effort than making a phone call or writing a letter, but a petition is a less powerful way to make a case unless you are sure to get enough signatures to represent a critical mass of support. I don't know of any formula for determining how many signatures it will take to be powerfully effective. In a small town or organization, 50 percent of the voting public might be both achievable and necessary. In a large city or campus, however, as low as 1 percent of the constituency could be an overwhelming showing. The committee should try to determine how many they believe they can realistically get and how many signatures would be necessary to have influence and set that number as a goal. Too few signatures could even backfire by making the library's interests appear to be "special interests."

Once you've set a goal for signatures, the core committee will have to enlist as many volunteers as possible to circulate petitions. The committee should decide on wording for the resolution of support. It needs to be clear, understandable, and unequivocal. Because the volunteers will be asking so many to sign, they will have to be able to explain exactly what the library is asking for and be able to answer questions. The resolution on the petition should reflect what the volunteer is telling them.

All volunteers should get a fact sheet to reproduce for handouts. The fact sheet should give the details of what the library needs and is asking for and what that means for funding, staffing, services, programs. Basic facts about the library should also be included. What is the current operating budget? How many people use the library and for what? When was the last time the library had a major increase for new construction? Be sure that your volunteers are armed with all the answers so they are not asked questions they can't answer.

Petition forms should be reproduced so that they all look the same. The petition needs to include space for a signature and an address. Ask each volunteer how many full pages he or she thinks she can get filled out, and then give each a few extras. Set a deadline for returns and then, if possible, have a member or members of the core committee follow up with the volunteers several days ahead of deadline to ensure that all is going well.

You can help volunteers by making suggestions for places to take the petition. Around the neighborhood or through the dorm are obvious choices, but consider less obvious places like the bookstore, the grocery store, a concert, church. Wherever the library constituents gather is a good place. If committee members are going to speak for the library at a service club, for example, ask them to take petitions with them for signing. The idea is to get as many signatures as possible to present to those who will make the decision regarding support for the library's plans.

Your trustees and Friends can maximize the value of the petition drive by turning the presentation of the petitions to the administration into a media event. If you have been successful in getting a large amount of grassroots support translated into signatures, it is likely that the local news media would be interested in covering the event. Plan to present the petitions in a public forum and ensure that you can provide a large audience. The committee that led the petition drive should let the media know that public statements will be made on behalf of the library and that petitions signed by hundreds or thousands of supporters will be handed over to the administration (or city council). Figure 5.7 is an example of a resolution of support.

POSTCARDS

A postcard campaign is somewhere between a letter-writing campaign and a petition drive in terms of difficulty and impact. While nothing will beat a well-stated personal letter and it's fairly easy to amass a long list of supporters via a petition, a postcard campaign encompasses the best elements of both.

Consider printing up hundreds or thousands of postcards with the library's message (what it is you are asking). On the message side of the postcard, you have the "I support" message. On the address side, you have the address of the person you wish to influence—the dean or the mayor, for example. To be truly effective, the postcards should also be prestamped or postpaid (a good investment for the Friends). Decide how many postcards will be needed to have a powerful impact and amass volunteers to hand them out.

As with the petition drive, the volunteers can hand postcards out wherever the library's constituents gather. Rather than asking for a signature on a petition, the volunteer asks that library supporters sign their names and include a brief message of support and drop the card in the mailbox. Like those circulating petitions, the volunteers need to be armed with all the pertinent information about the library's request and about the current status of library services.

Figures 5.8 and 5.9 are examples of campaign postcards.

Resolution Supporting 1% for Norfolk Public Library

Whereas the Norfolk Public Library connects children and adults with books, computers, and other resources they need to live, learn and prosper in a global society, and;

Whereas the Norfolk Public Library educates and promotes understanding of diverse cultures in our city, and;

Whereas the Norfolk Public Library contributes to the quality of life for all residents in all neighborhoods, and;

Whereas Norfolk Public Library resources support the creation of new businesses, new business opportunities, and new jobs thereby enhancing the economic base of the city, and;

Whereas nearly 70% of all Norfolk residents have library cards and use the library on a regular basis, and;

Whereas everyone benefits from a more literate community supported by a good public library, and;

Whereas funding for libraries is an investment in the future of all our youth, and in the intellectual growth of all people, and;

Whereas funding for the Norfolk Public Library, traditionally at or above 1% of the city's operating budget, dropped below 1% in 1992 and has stayed below 1%;

Therefore be it resolved that we, the undersigned, fully support a return of direct funding for libraries in the City of Norfolk to 1% of the city's operating budget.

Figure 5.7—Resolution for petition drive, Norfolk (Va.) Public Library.

This resolution is designed to be the "cover" page for a petition drive. It clearly states what the petitioners are asking and why it matters.

It's time to

Thrive!

Norfolk Public Library

It's time to Thrive!

As a Norfolk citizen who uses and
benefits from the public library,
I support additional funding for
libraries in the amount of $1 million
for fiscal year 2000.

Mayor John Doe
100 Main Street
Any City, USA 12345

Name: _____

Attn: _____

Address: _____

_____

Figure 5.8—Postcard to support operating budget, Norfolk (Va.) Public Library.

Postcards are easy and inexpensive to produce and can be sent en masse to influence decision makers. A postcard campaign works best when postcards are prestamped so advocates don't hesitate to sign them and drop them in the mail.

Remember...

1%

for Libraries

Friends of the Norfolk
Public Library
PO Box 3234
Norfolk, Virginia 23514

Non. Profit Org.
U.S. Postage
PAID
Norfolk, VA
Permit No. 2112

There's Still Time to Help the Library!

It's time to thrive in Norfolk! Your phone call will make a difference. **Please take just one minute of your time today to make one phone call to the Office of the Mayor at 664-4679 and voice your support for 1% for Libraries.**

If you have already called, thank you for your continued support of our libraries.
If you have any questions, please feel free to contact Hannah Brewer at 489-4746.

Figure 5.9—Reminder postcard, Norfolk (Va.) Public Library.

This postcard is especially designed to remind advocates to make a phone call to register their library support and thanks those who've already done so.

TELEPHONE CAMPAIGN

Numbers count, so finding easy ways to get large numbers of people to register their support for libraries should be as creative as possible. Oftentimes you can get a lot of people to make a phone call to the decision makers—if you make it easy. One effective campaign idea is to wage a campaign designed to get as many calls as possible to the office of the mayor or dean or whoever has ultimate power over the library's budget or plans.

A phone campaign must include broad public education about what the library is asking for and why. Using the Friends mailing list, newsletter, and op-ed opportunities, the Friends and trustees should begin to get the word out. Let everyone know what the library needs and what they can do to help—in other words make that phone call.

PAID NEWSPAPER ADVERTISING

In addition to sending flyers to the Friends' members and other supporters, consider a newspaper ad. It, too, can be a highly effective way to get supporters to influence decision makers. Working with the paper's ad department or depending on help from a talented Friend, design an eye-catching advertisement that tells the reading public what the library wants, why, and how they can help by making one phone call. Be sure to include the office phone number of the person you wish them to call. Also, to make the phone call easier, give them the one sentence or phrase to use in making the call, for example, "Tell the Mayor you support 1% for libraries."

If you can afford it, plan to place two or three ads to run intermittently during the course of the campaign. This way you will remind everyone to call (even those whom you haven't identified as library supporters—using the newspaper really makes this a broad-based campaign). In addition, a large display ad will catch the eyes of the decision makers and add that much more pressure to your request for support.

As with all promotional materials, the ads should be fully paid for by the Friends or other library support group and this fact should be clearly stated in the ad. The Friends might wish to make a paid advertisement pay off for them in another way. If the ad includes a clip-and-send membership form, they may well be able to swell their own ranks, which will both build on the advocacy network they have developed and help them build resources to continue financial support of the library.

Figure 5.10 is an example of such an advertisement.

Remember...

1%

for Libraries

It's Time to Thrive in Norfolk!

<u>One voice can make a difference</u>. The city of Norfolk's budget for fiscal year 2001 is being planned now. Let the City Council know that our libraries are important. **Please take just one minute of your time to make one phone call to the Office of the Mayor by February 28 at 664-4679 and voice your support for 1% for libraries.** Your one phone call will make a difference.

Historically, the city has funded libraries at or above 1% of its budget. In fiscal year 1992 that funding level dropped. Now libraries are funded at approximately 0.8%. The Friends of the Norfolk Public Library along with the Board of Trustees are asking that the city of Norfolk restore 1% of its operating budget for libraries for the new fiscal year. One percent for libraries would raise the annual operating budget from the current $4.8 million per year to $6 million per year.

Paid for by the Friends of the Norfolk Public Library.

Figure 5.10—Newspaper display advertisement, Norfolk (Va.) Public Library.

A bold, eye-catching advertisement telling readers that "one voice can make a difference" is a good investment of Friends' or supporters' funds. This ad also tells supporters exactly what they can do to help.

E-MAIL CAMPAIGN

As the use of e-mail becomes more ubiquitous, it becomes an increasingly effective method for communicating. Even today, however, the protocol for its use is still a little fuzzy and many people genuinely resent being "spammed." Probably no one is going to enjoy getting hundreds of phone calls, letters, or postcards putting pressure on for a specific decision, but getting hundreds or thousands of e-mails will probably be even more annoying (to understate it!).

There is always a fine line in any public pressure campaign between registering a high level of support for your cause and really making those in positions of power mad at those promoting the library's agenda. The library itself will suffer from a campaign that goes too far and generates anger and mistrust. Remember, even though you are working to address a specific need in the short term, the library staff and trustees will have to work with the same decision makers in the future and in an ongoing way. It's important that, in waging any kind of campaign, you not end up winning the battle but losing the war.

Unless you are absolutely sure that e-mail would be a reasonable approach, I don't really recommend attempting to send hundreds or thousands of advocate messages. This doesn't mean that e-mail won't be useful, however. Key members of the library's support group can certainly use e-mail as one way to correspond with the administration about the library's campaign and the library's goals.

MEDIA EVENT

A very public campaign that includes letters to the editor, paid advertisements, postcards, and letters will probably attract the attention of the local news media. Great! The more free (and "objective") coverage you get about the campaign the better. Because media coverage is important, you may want to work to create a media event around the campaign.

A "hook" for the media is a kick-off rally. The kick-off, obviously, is an event designed to generate enthusiasm and interest in the campaign itself. To make it newsworthy and, therefore, a media event, you should try to include remarks from VIPs in the community who support the cause. Any kind of programmatic component you can think of will also help. Be sure to let the media know well in advance (you may even want to gauge their interest and find out from them what it would take to get their coverage). If you are working to get television coverage make sure that something about the event has visual interest—again important people or a local celebrity would be good. The paper will probably be an easier sell than television, because they will be interested that a major campaign is afoot for the library but they will not be concerned that something be there for the camera.

FOLLOWING UP

Throughout the targeted campaign it's important that you keep the pressure on all your supporters to take action. As much as constituents care about the library and support the library's agenda, taking action may not be on the top of a busy person's list of things to do. There are some simple ways you can remind your supporters to take a moment and make a call, send a letter, or send an e-mail message.

Reminders of some sort should follow a week or so after the initial push. This way the campaign objectives are still fairly fresh in supporters' minds. Also, you don't want to extend the campaign very long, because if it is too dispersed, it will lose the intensity of its effect. Phone calls by the core committee are certainly effective to remind supporters, but they are also time-consuming. Mailing reminders work well. If you send a letter, you might include a preprinted Post-it note stating the action needed and the deadline; the letter can say simply, "Just a reminder, the library needs your help. Please post this note on your refrigerator to remind you to make that call (send that letter, etc.)." A postcard is cheaper and easier to send (no stuffing envelopes), and with both the letter and the postcard you can take the opportunity to thank supporters for their support.

Figure 5.9 is an example of a postcard sent to supporters.

An even more effective approach (but possibly more costly) is to take out a half-page advertisement in the local paper reminding supporters that you need their help and urging them to take action. Figure 5.11 is a good example. Such an ad has the dual benefit of reminding people *and* sending the message to the decision makers that library supporters are serious. Though display ads are expensive, they are a tremendously effective way to send your message across the city or campus. They are highly visible and they will be seen by and may influence those who have never even thought about the library before.

Remember...
1%
for Libraries

There's Still Time to Help the Library!

One voice can make a difference. The city of Norfolk's budget for fiscal year 2001 is being planned now. Let the City Council know that our libraries are important. **Please take just one minute of your time to make one phone call to the Office of the Mayor at 664-4679 and voice your support for 1% for libraries.** Your one phone call will make a difference.

Historically, the city has funded libraries at or above 1% of its budget. In fiscal year 1992 that funding level dropped. Now libraries are funded at approximately 0.8%. The Friends of the Norfolk Public Library along with the Board of Trustees are asking that the city of Norfolk restore 1% of its operating budget for libraries for the new fiscal year. One percent for libraries would raise the annual operating budget from the current $4.8 million per year to $6 million per year.

Paid for by the Friends of the Norfolk Public Library.

Figure 5.11—Newspaper display advertisement, Norfolk (Va.) Public Library.

This reminder ad carries forward the same look and theme as Figure 5.9 and, therefore, is a strong recognizable reminder. The bold look and short caption says it all.

SAYING THANK YOU

Win, lose or draw, it is important that you thank everyone who was involved in the effort and especially that you keep the channels of communication open with those in power. You can effectively say thank you with a final letter to the editor from the chairperson of the campaign committee.

An article in the Friends' newsletter is also important. Let the Friends know the outcome of the campaign and analyze the results for them— why it worked, how the Friends and library supporters can continue to work for the library's agenda. Keep the tone upbeat, even if the library did not prevail, because you want to be able to generate enthusiasm next time around and not make your advocates feel like the library is a lost cause.

It's also a very good idea—if you lose—for the presidents of the Friends and of the trustees to write to the final decision makers to let them know you appreciate their consideration of your concerns and to restate why the library's agenda is so important. If you win final support, don't gloat. Let those who finally made it happen know how much you appreciate their support. Promise them that their decision will be one they can be proud of and that hundreds or thousands of library supporters join you in your appreciation.

However big and important this campaign, the fact remains that advocacy for the library will continue. A new building or a large operating increase does not mean your job is done. Advocacy is an ongoing effort. Remember the message—why is your library important to the community it serves? How does it support the goals of the larger organization? Continue to keep the library's message present in everything you publish and every speech you make.

We live in a highly political and competitive world. If we as librarians and as individuals continue to be outspoken and effective advocates, the day may come when libraries are universally regarded as critical components of our cities and institutions worthy of full support. Until that day arrives, it's our job to continue to remind people that libraries are unique institutions safe-guarding individual learning opportunities, research, literacy, intellectual growth, and our democracy itself. We have a cause. We must be champions of it.

6 FINAL THOUGHTS

In the end, an extremely important message for all library advocates is to persevere. Hang in there because making the case for your library may take years and even when you feel that your library is a top priority with your campus or community administration, priorities for the people in charge change and the library will always be vulnerable.

It has been said that the race to getting what you want from the powers that be is a marathon, not a sprint. How true. To be an effective advocate you will need to educate the community about the importance of libraries—why library services matter to them. You will need to harness and organize grassroots support. You will need to be sure that there are strong connections on a personal level between yourself, your trustees, your Friends, and the people who have power in your community or on your campus. You will need to be sure that your public relations efforts are focused on getting support for the library and its services, not just on increasing use. But the truth is, even if you do all of this, and do it well, you will not always get everything you want every time.

MEASURING SUCCESS

A simple way to know if you are being successful is to measure the results of a specific campaign against what you were after in the first place. If you were working to get information policy changed and the policy that you wrote and championed was accepted without revision, you will know you were 100 percent successful. If you asked for a $1 million increase to your operating budget and you got it, obviously the measurement is easy. In reality, however, you will not always get what you ask for (or get what you need!). In fact, if your requests are being fully met on a routine basis, I would question whether you are asking enough. More often you will get some portion of what you were after or even none at all. Does that mean you were 100 percent unsuccessful? Not at all.

Within the context of a long-term, ongoing campaign to raise the profile and importance of the library in the community's or establishment's eyes, you may have made significant headway that is not (yet) measurable in terms of dollars or policy support. Every new connection you make with a potential supporter who has influence in your community is a win. Every additional voice among grassroots support is a step closer to meeting your goal. Every bit of "ink" your library gets from the press increases your profile and will make your next campaign that much easier.

Many samples of the Norfolk Public Library's 1 percent campaign have been used in this book. I wish I could report that our library did, indeed, get the full additional funding that 1 percent of the city's operating budget would have equaled. We didn't. We got a little more than half of what we were asking. Did we fail? To be honest, it sure felt like it at first, but after a chance to lick our wounds a bit, we were able to post some significant gains in our campaign and begin to understand how successful we really were.

To begin with, while we did not get 100 percent of our request for the operating budget, our campaign put significant pressure on the city council, and our plans and long-awaited funding for new building received full support. We were accorded the capital funds for the first time in over 15 years to design a new anchor branch. Furthermore, significant funds were placed in our city's facilities budget restricted to *the library* to enhance our buildings and market our collections and services.

The most significant gain in the campaign, however, came in a form other than money, which bodes well for long-term support. One of the candidates running for election to city council ran on a platform that included, specifically, his support for 1 percent funding for the Norfolk Public Library. His support was strong and unequivocal. He took out two full-page ads in our local newspaper expressing his support, and in all his campaign literature he included a statement of his belief that the library should be supported at no less than 1 percent of the city's operating budget. Even though this candidate was the decided underdog, he won. Did his stand on libraries turn the tide? Who knows? Library supporters aren't sure but then neither are the sitting council members who saw as plainly as anyone that the winning candidate included support for libraries as a distinguishing campaign issue and won. Now we have a new member of city council who fully and openly supports our agenda, and we have six other council members (who will all face reelection at some point) wondering if support for libraries put him over the top.

In addition to winning a candidate over to our side, the 1 percent campaign generated over 500 phone calls in a very short period of time to the mayor's office. That kind of active support is extremely rare. Short of a long-term moratorium on garbage collection, it's hard to imagine 500 people calling about any specific city service over the course of just two weeks. Although it didn't secure the full 1 percent increase, the campaign made grassroots support of the library well known. As an added bonus, many of the people who were compelled to call also decided to join the Friends for the first time.

Asking for 1 percent of the city's budget (or an increase of $1 million) was a real stretch. It would have meant a 20 percent increase in the library's budget. Was it a realistic expectation? We can only guess that had we asked for less, we would have gotten even less. As it was, this ambitious campaign netted us a fairly significant increase in our library's budget, commitment to and funding for our capital building plans, and a new city council member who is outspoken in his support for library funding!

Sometimes you will have to measure success by what you've learned in a campaign that wasn't fully successful. When you work hard and put a lot of effort into a campaign, it's extremely difficult to accept defeat, whether that means a level-funded budget, a budget cut, or a lost referendum. Remember, though, that advocacy for library support is a long-term endeavor. In fact, apart from an occasional hiatus, it is probably safe to assume that political advocacy is as much a part of the successful library director's position description as any other component of the job.

Understanding this means that even failure is an opportunity to increase your chances for future success. It's important that following a "failed" campaign, you and your trustees, Friends, and staff members spend time analyzing what worked, and especially what didn't. This is a real opportunity to refine your message and refine your approach. In fact, if you have failed at passing a referendum, you may want to take time to survey the public and find out what would encourage their support of the library in future referendums. A real learning opportunity.

KEEP YOUR EYES ON THE PRIZE

Your job is to ensure that the library is a priority with those who make final decisions regarding policy and funding, and that all your political efforts are geared toward meeting this goal. In reality, funding priorities change, emergencies come up, and sometimes someone else competing for a larger piece of the same pie makes a more compelling case. The hardest part of being an effective advocate may well be sticking with it even when the results of your efforts are not readily apparent. If you are doing everything you can to make the case for the library on an ongoing basis, you *are* being effective. One thing for sure, if you make it easy for those in power to solve funding problems at the expense of the library, they absolutely will.

Even though you may not win every battle, you can win long-term by ensuring that libraries are seen as critical. Good, effective advocacy can ensure that the administration and those who fund libraries or develop policy understand that excellent library service furthers their own agenda and does so with an exceedingly small percentage of an overall operating budget. That doesn't mean cuts won't be made from time to time, but it can mean that those cuts are made with great reluctance and a true understanding that there will be a negative consequence as a result.

I would add "energy, commitment, and stamina" to a list of requirements for any library director in today's competitive environment—or maybe our environment has always been competitive, but the requirements for offering effective library service were far fewer and less sophisticated in days gone by. Or, could it be that those old stereotypical librarians—often referred to as "battle-axes"—knew something we are just beginning to rediscover? Maybe they understood that good library service is worth fighting for determinedly and without apology. Whatever the case, we can't shy away from our obligation to ensure that we have the tools and support we need to deliver the kind of library service that is critical to our communities. It's a long-term commitment for us; in fact, it's an essential part of the job.

INDEX

ABOUT THE AUTHOR

Sally Gardner Reed is currently the director of the Norfolk Public Library in Virginia. She has also directed and advocated for libraries in New Hampshire, Vermont, and Iowa. Reed is the recent recipient of the Herbert and Virginia White Award for promoting librarianship. She has conducted dozens of advocacy training workshops across the country for librarians, Friends groups, and trustees. Reed is passionate about libraries and believes they will always be a critical component of a free society's landscape—especially if librarians and supporters are successful in making the case!